MM

DEADLOCK

Dublin vs Meath 1991

DEADLOCK

Dublin vs Meath 1991

EOGHAN CORRY ∽

Gill & Macmillan

Gill & Macmillan
Hume Avenue, Park West, Dublin 12
with associated companies throughout the world
www.gillmacmillan.ie

© Eoghan Corry 2011
978 07171 4814 1

Index compiled by Cover to Cover
Typography design by Make Communication
Print origination by O'K Graphic Design, Dublin
Printed and bound by ScandBook, Sweden

This book is typeset in 12/15 pt Minion

The paper used in this book comes from the
wood pulp of managed forests. For every tree
felled, at least one tree is planted, thereby
renewing natural resources.

A CIP catalogue record for this book is available
from the British Library.

5 4 3 2 1

For Páraic, Fergal and Cillian,
and in memory of Ciarán Corry, 1957–2011, who
brought me on the pillion of his Honda 175 on
24 August 1975 to stand on Hill 16 and witness
the events described on pages 95–6.

CONTENTS

PROLOGUE: THE SOD   IX

1.   Gael force '91   1
2.   Italia '90   25
3.   Changing game   42
4.   Rules of engagement   61
5.   Players and watchers   84
6.   Sequence of events   99
7.   Aftermath   146
8.   Epilogue   185

     THE RECORDS   186
     APPENDIX: THE SPEECHES   192
     INDEX   194

| PROLOGUE

The sod

The forecast was for rain, but the rain never fell. Instead the sun shone, and the warming breeze of early summer passed over north Dublin, whisking its way in the gaps between the Hogan and Cusack Stands and the ageing, ramshackle terracing of Croke Park along the banks of the Royal Canal, past a sod of earth ten feet out from the canal goal.

The grass on Ireland's most important sports field was looking threadbare at places, and groundsman Paddy Walsh was worried. Hard ground means grazed elbows, and there was only so much could be done with that surface to make it green and soft again. For Paddy and his predecessor, Con Ó Laoire, the solution was canal water, pumped through the gates and under the terracing by the fire brigade from the nearby Royal Canal. And lots of sand. But somehow Paddy didn't get to water that sod.

Saturday came and the rain never fell, and when the crowds began trickling into the stadium at midday on Sunday there was still no sign of it.

They were coming in growing numbers to see Dublin and Meath do battle in the first round of the Leinster championship, unaware that these teams were about to make a piece of history that would be remembered long after their exploits, their medals and their trophied sideboards were forgotten.

The spectators too would have been surprised if they were told this was to become a major event in the cultural life of Ireland, for this wasn't a memorable football match, either for the skills on show or for the crunching limbs and bones, which had given contests between these counties a sort of testosterone infamy over the previous eight years.

Mick Lyons didn't know it as he tried to solo out of the Dublin defence, P. J. Gillic didn't know it as he retrieved the ball and sent it in, to drop a few yards short of the goal, John O'Leary didn't know it as he raced clear of the goal, attempting to catch Gillic's uncharacteristically aimless lob.

Neither spectators nor players knew it as they skipped a collective heartbeat, saw as one that O'Leary wasn't going to make it, that the ball was going to evade his grasping hands and drop behind him into the unguarded goalmouth.

And onto that sod it landed—for one moment the driest, bounciest sod in Ireland—to soar off again in the direction of the empty Dublin goal.

What would happen next? If it went under the bar it counted as three points and Meath were into the next round. If it went over the bar it was one point, the match would be a draw and the whole drama would have to be re-enacted a week later. Under the Cusack Stand, Dublin's team manager, Paddy Cullen, was sure that the longish grass in the goalmouth would deaden the bounce and that it would drop into the net. 'It must have hit a hard spot,' he decided, as he watched it climb.

The height of a Gaelic football goalpost is 2.5 metres: eight feet, two inches. The ball, that 380 grams of pressurised air, eighteen panels in all, two trapezoidal groups and one rectangular group, encased in leather and emblazoned with an O'Neills logo, paused for what seemed like an eternity before it timed its leap skyward.

The world turned as that ball ascended into history. It

glided towards the post, climbed, paused as if it was about to change its mind and, just at the critical moment, began moving again, eight foot, eight foot four inches and over. John O'Leary had come off the line to cover Tommy Dowd and didn't see it go over the bar. He heard the roar of the crowd, which told him Meath had scored. But it wasn't the roar of a goal.

Over the bar. A draw. Come back next week. Ladies and gentlemen, the show is not over.

Hours after the match ended the rain came. The driest sod in Ireland turned soggy. No ball like this would bounce over the bar again all summer or for many years to come in the sacred soil of Páirc an Chrócaigh.

Chapter 1

GAEL FORCE '91

Change comes slowly within the GAA. *The Association is a democracy within a democracy within a democracy.*

—PETER QUINN, incoming GAA president

The GAA congress of 1991 more closely resembled those of 1951 or 1961 than that of 1971, which dropped its ban on 'foreign games' (which really meant the competing football codes of soccer and rugby and the stick-and-ball game of hockey), or that of 1981, when an innovative solution was found to the handpass debate. The summer after Italia '90 the delegates were in no mood for reforming anything.

The director-general, Liam Mulvihill, warned the four hundred delegates that the Government had decided that Croke Park could not be the site for the new national stadium but should be used for Gaelic games. The rules of the GAA didn't allow for the playing of 'certain other field games' in Croke Park. GAA members had always looked at Croke Park as their national stadium and as the symbolic headquarters of the organisation for nearly a century.

There was one issue buzzing around the room in the Burlington Hotel. Pat Fanning, former president of the association, said it was 'a nettle that was stinging in many counties.' It was the new policy of paying managers of football teams.

Dublin's Donal Hickey proposed that sponsors' logos

should be allowed on playing jerseys, and, surprisingly, the motion got the required two-thirds majority, 194 to 96. Con Clarke, the Dublin chairman, assured delegates that it wouldn't look like the Candy or Sharp logos on English soccer shirts. There was a limit of 100 square centimetres on the size of the logo. Frank Murphy, the Cork secretary, said it would be cheap and commercial to emblazon them on jerseys.

Longford called for inter-county players to be eligible to represent the counties of their parents' and grandparents' birth.

The congress decided to formally complain to RTE about the quality of inter-county television coverage.

The GAA swore in a new president. Peter Quinn of Co. Fermanagh spoke in familiar, almost formulaic terms of how he was motivated by the radicalism that infused the association in the early years and was enamoured of the resilience it showed in the War of Independence but regretted that much had been lost. However, he was a business consultant, used to the world of finance amid the cacophony of schoolteachers who ran the association. He talked about the loss of 'market share' (a minuscule 7 per cent in Dublin), about the need for the GAA to become more innovative and entrepreneurial instead of being hindered by progressively bureaucratic structures, and about how its image was

negative, defensive and excessively conservative and backward . . . I look forward to the day when those adjectives are replaced by their opposites. I wonder what is the opposite of defensive. In this context it can hardly be offensive.

Quinn wasn't joking. He had identified serious organisational deficiencies within an association that had grown complacent according as it had grown old and dominant in sporting life. It wasn't just the Heath-Robinson decision-making process, with motions presented at a club AGM then presented to a county convention and sent forward to a committee of ex-presidents for inclusion on the clár at Congress, proposed and seconded and voted on by an assembly of delegates who never had to listen to the debate or justify their decision. One county secretary brought his twelve-year-old son to vote, in the absence of one of the registered delegates.

The association's continual attempts to run a major national organisation from the equivalent of a political party conference or an ard-fheis had bequeathed to the 1990s GAA a messy pottage of rules and policies.

Some of the dafter rules, voted through in the rushes of pious enthusiasm that sometimes grip the GAA's annual congress, had been discarded by 1991, including one that insisted on official correspondence being on Irish watermarked paper. Others, such as the insistence on Irish-language team lists, had been retained and were still the grounds of post-match objections. One technical foul, the taking of a kick-out from the wrong spot by a goalkeeper, had two separate and contradictory penalties in the rulebook, inserted in different periods. The rulebook was vulnerable to a well-argued legal challenge, as would increasingly become the case in the 1990s.

The major problem facing the association was indecision. The committee structures and the chain of command among the full-time executive staff of twenty-three made decision-making cumbersome and unworkable. At the centre of it all was the elite of schoolteachers who had been running the GAA for generations. There was a shortage of management skills and business acumen and even of an awareness of what a modern sporting association should be.

This was the state of the GAA in 1991.

All-Ireland semi-finals don't attract the neutrals as they did in the past.

—LIAM MULVIHILL's report to Congress, 1991

Much as they liked to believe otherwise, the GAA executive at Croke Park hadn't even got sole control of their own games. The big money, the real power was still to be found in the provinces.

The most powerful units of the association were the provincial councils of Connacht, Leinster, Munster and Ulster, which had been merrily running its day-to-day affairs for ninety years. Croke Park fretted over standards of discipline and winter national league fixtures in drab shed-like venues, but it was the provincial councils that made most of the decisions. They were given autonomy on virtually all matters and had an income-generating power well in excess of anything Croke Park possessed.

Croke Park had to subsist on a diet of the all-Ireland finals, a hurling semi-final and two football semi-finals. Leinster had ten annual football championship fixtures and three hurling championship fixtures. Munster had effectually three football championship fixtures, of which only one was capable of generating income, but it had the consolation of four lucrative hurling fixtures and the choice of four stadiums each with a capacity of 50,000 in which to fix them. Ulster had eight football fixtures and a predictable 30,000 attendance at the final. Connacht had to subsist on four football fixtures.

It was to the provincial level that counties looked for guidance on finance, including the much sought-after grants for grounds development, and on disciplinary matters. They also had a legacy of practices and customs inherited from long-forgotten council decisions. Leinster even had a fund for the repair of historic churches, which was deftly used by Jack Boothman for the repair of disintegrating Church of Ireland parish churches.

The provincial structure had helped the GAA survive in times of crisis, including during the War of Independence, the Civil War and the armed conflict in Ulster. But it also managed to stall progress on any flights of fancy by the Central Council, and this opposition endangered the Cusack Stand project in 1938, the Ceannáras in 1984 and even the redevelopment of Croke Park in 1993.

Few disciplinary clampdowns, of which there were many emanating from Central Council sub-committees in the 1980s and 1990s, carried enough armour-plating to make it past the perils of a lively Ulster Council debate.

The provinces retained their power as long as their income models, the provincial championships, survived intact. Hence most motions proposing an open draw perished at the congress before they were even put to the vote.

The GAA was eventually to break free of the stranglehold imposed by its own provincial councils after shadow all-Ireland championships were introduced in 1997 in hurling and 2001 in football. In the meantime it was also entitled to television income. In 1991 this source of income was to become extremely significant.

———

Meath failed to learn the lesson that you can win the hard way and yet be nice to everyone in victory. Some of the players are unable to handle the media properly.

—TOMMY CARR

Nor had the media changed much in their approach to the games over the previous decades. The reports were quaint, twee and deferential, products of a print media whose relationship with the association had changed little in the decades since the first full-time sports writers were employed.

Ireland had been at the forefront in the establishment of sports journalism in the nineteenth century, and the GAA was a major beneficiary of this. Michael Cusack, P. P. Sutton and Frank Dineen, while not full-time journalists, had used access to the print media to promote the association. The first GAA full-time correspondents had emerged in the 1920s: enthusiastic part-timers Paddy Mehigan from Cork (a civil servant who acted as GAA stringer for the *Cork Examiner* and *Irish Times* and was the GAA's first radio commentator), P. J. Devlin from Newry (a friend of Cusack's who wrote in turn for the *Catholic Bulletin, Evening Herald, Freeman's Journal* and *Evening Telegraph* and was the first GAA correspondent of the *Irish Press*), James Bolger from Oilgate, Co. Wexford (a civil servant who wrote in the *Irish Independent* under the pen-name Recorder) and Seán Bonner from Donegal (an insurance executive) reported the matches on Sundays for the daily newspapers. Mitchell Cogley, later sports editor of the *Irish Independent*, father of the RTE head of sport Fred Cogley and grandfather of another RTE head of sport, Niall Cogley, assisted Devlin at the 1931 all-Ireland final and was an enthusiastic columnist. Each was from a GAA background and brought with him a largely enthusiastic analysis of GAA affairs.

They were replaced by sub-editors from the sports departments (or even news departments) who spent their Sundays writing match reports: John D. Hickey (from 1948) and Pádraig Puirséil (from 1951). In 1959 Mick Dunne, a full-time writer who had come through the copy-boy system, became the *Irish Press* full-time GAA correspondent. In 1963 Paddy Downey joined the *Sunday Review* and then the *Irish Times* as a full-time GAA correspondent. In the *Irish Independent* Donal Carroll and then Donal Keenan succeeded Hickey; Puirséil succeeded Mick Dunne on his departure to RTE in 1971; and Peadar O'Brien succeeded Puirséil as GAA correspondent in 1979. Peadar was also moonlighting for an English newspaper, the *Sun*, as Tommy · Fitzgerald. (When the *Irish Press* folded in 1995 and O'Brien's by-line was used by the *Sun* for the first time, the *Irish Press* chapel of the National Union of Journalists passed a motion of condolence to poor Tommy Fitzgerald on the loss of his job.) Val Dorgan and then Jim O'Sullivan took over the GAA correspondent role at the *Examiner,* which had been occupied by Paddy Mehigan. Paddy O'Hara became the *Irish News* GAA correspondent and Liam McDowell occupied a similar role for the *Belfast Telegraph* and Denis O'Hara for the *News Letter* (Belfast).

The allocation of press accreditation under the old system was a relatively unsophisticated procedure. The GAA's general secretary, Paddy O'Keeffe, and then Seán Ó Síocháin allocated four press passes for the national newspapers, and the radio commentator Mícheál O'Hehir was allocated a commentary box on a precarious wooden pylon at the Hogan Stand side of the ground for the few occasions on which a live broadcast was allowed (basically for Railway Cup finals, two or three provincial finals and the five matches in the all-Ireland series).

By the 1970s this had evolved into a system of A-passes for the four national correspondents and B-passes for the growing number of writers who were arriving to cover ancillary issues, the minor match, dressing-room quotations and 'colour' pieces. Gerry McCarthy of the *Irish Press,* Seán Óg Ó Ceallacháin of the *Evening Press,* Aidan McCarthy (briefly) and then Seán Kilfeather of the *Irish Times*, Paddy Hickey of the *Evening Herald*, Michael Ellard of the *Cork Examiner*, Michael Fortune of the *Irish Press* and a new breed of reporters recruited by Adhamhnán O'Sullivan in 1980 were the most prominent of these. Among them were Vincent Hogan, who had served his apprenticeship with the Hayter's Teamwork sports agency in London, Martin Breheny from the *Tuam Herald* and David Walsh from the *Leitrim Observer*.

The recruitment of Adhamhnán's team and the founding of the *Sunday Tribune*, with the innovative Séamus Martin as sports editor, in November 1980, together injected a new energy into what was a moribund sector, ill-informed and nepotistic, dominated by single-source stories and age-old conventions. Teams were announced on Tuesday nights and published alongside fixtures in Wednesday's newspapers. The quotations wrote themselves, as players repeated the clichés they had read in their childhood. When they were not mundane enough, reporters often made them up with the connivance of the interviewees: fifty-fifty chances and breaks of the ball at midfield. The arbitrary and petty way in which managers were punished for being critical of match officials added to the absence of any adventurousness on the part of interviewer and interviewee alike.

By 1991 two *Sunday Tribune* journalists were also on the B-pass list, Seán Moran and Tom Humphries, whose quest for sports-writing Zen hadn't been dented by the fact that he lasted less than a month in John Horgan's new postgraduate course in journalism in DCU.

Maintaining a healthy distance from the jargon of the press benches was the most iconic figure of all, Con Houlihan, a giant, soft-spoken Kerryman (the *Sunday Tribune* once proposed that he be made an honorary Alp) with a poetic style derived from extensive reading of

American literature. He always stood in the same place in the canal end, and Seán Doherty once said that his only shot at goal during his Dublin career was so off target that 'he almost hit Con Houlihan.' Though Houlihan's remark in 1978 that Paddy Cullen ran back into his goalmouth like a woman who smelt a cake burning was to become his best known, there were thousands of others, many of them in the back-page columns about the 1991 Deadlock series that he wrote for the *Evening Press* before retiring at 8 a.m. to Mulligan's of Poolbeg Street for his aperitif of whiskey and milk.

In his coverage of the Dublin-Meath Deadlock he mentions that he has seen Fellini's *La Strada* seven times, refers to Carson McCullers's *The Ballad of the Sad Café* and quotes D. H. Lawrence's remark that 'the only tragedy is loss of heart.' His summation of the event: 'All Gaeldom looked on agog.'

The great man ('In truth, I am not a journalist—but I work for a newspaper') was facing a tragedy of his own, worthy of the closing scenes of *La Strada*. Houlihan's newspaper, many suspected, was doomed. The Irish Press Group was facing a set of problems whose intractability and nastiness would have overwhelmed a gifted businessman. The three titles of the group closed suddenly in 1995.

——

There is a small group of soft-centred, soft-natured people who have absolutely no knowledge of the GAA. Included in that grouping is a large slice of our national media.

—LIAM HAYES

In 1975 the GAA appointed a full-time public-relations officer, Pat Quigley, and when he returned as sports editor of the

Sunday World in 1985 he was succeeded by Danny Lynch, a press officer in the Office of Public Works.

Lynch was used to crisis management, and he had several to manage during his tenure, which he handled successfully. Only Lynch could manage the scandal of Tommy Dowd, the all-Ireland winning-team captain, and team-mate Graham Geraghty being turned away from an after-match function, complete with the Sam Maguire cup, because they hadn't got the correct invitations in their hands.

Lynch also took the business of press accreditation to hand. Tickets under previous media regimes had tended to go astray: there were many beneficiaries of lax policing of the media accreditation. Not under Lynch.

The media interest in Gaelic games was low-key, except for the all-Ireland finals, when each of the provincial papers was sent a ticket. Some of these were snapped up by the provincial newspaper editors, but mostly the GAA correspondents were able to work with good access to matches and to dressing-rooms for post-match quotations.

Not that these were up to much. Journalists were in despair of getting the media-resistant and often shy players to say anything noteworthy. Even if the clichés were improving, they were being recycled. 'When you lose to Dublin there is no compensation' was attributed to more than one Meath player during the Deadlock of 1991.

By international standards the GAA stars had little to say, except occasionally when a Sunday newspaper splashed out £300 for a three-part series in which they would reveal all the secrets of the dressing-room.

The revolution began in Co. Meath. There was surprise and delight when Liam Hayes moved from the *Meath Chronicle* to the *Sunday Press* in 1985. Seán Boylan pleaded with the *Sunday Press* sports editor, Michael Carwood, not to let Liam write anything about Meath in the newspaper. Liam was prepared to write about them but revealed very little about his own or the team's psychology in his weekly columns. It was left to David Walsh of the rival *Sunday Tribune* to write a revealing piece about Hayes's tragic brother, who took his own life at a young age some years earlier, which was published on the day of the 1987 all-Ireland final.

In 1988 Walsh approached Colm O'Rourke to write an article for the following week's *Sunday Tribune* about the niggly and nasty all-Ireland final that Meath had just played with Cork and drawn. O'Rourke's first appearance was a hit (although he didn't write the memorable headline 'In the heat of battle—Nice guys finish last': that was the work of the high priest of *Tribune* headline-writing, Ger Siggins), and he was brought on to write a weekly column in 1991. Two Meath players were therefore writing opinion pieces in the newspapers during Deadlock. They subtly put their team's case and moved the psychological game to a new level, especially O'Rourke, who was unused to the protocol of newspaper work.

The public loved the glimpse of locker-room life. Nicknames for players entered GAA vocabulary: David Beggy was now referred to as 'Jinksy' by supporters as well as by his playing colleagues. It was also managed in a subtle way. O'Rourke devoted part of one of his Deadlock columns in the *Sunday Tribune* to how Mick Deegan would never forget missing possession in the first drawn match, which led to Meath's equalising score. It was a subtle way of putting extra pressure on the opposition.

RTE give scant coverage to GAA after the all-Ireland final while giving coverage to a club league competition organised by another code.

—LIAM MULVIHILL, Report to Congress, 1991

Broadcasting was at the beginning of a rapid evolution. RTE had anchored its radio coverage on a solid base: the unique qualities of Micheál Ó Muircheartaigh, later included in the *Guinness Book of Records* for an unbroken career in commentary, from 1949 to 2010.

His broadcasting technique was distinctive and unique, reflecting the old storytelling tradition rather than the conventions of running play descriptions in received English accents. In the middle of the 1992 all-Ireland final commentary he took a moment during a break in play to name the Four Masters, who compiled their Annals in Co. Donegal.

He followed a proud RTE heritage. In 1926 its predecessor, 2RN, was the first station outside the United States to broadcast a field sports event. Only four commentators had seized the microphone since: the irrepressible P. D. Mehigan, whose Cork accent became the subject of mimicry by Jimmy O'Dea; the nationalist orator Éamonn de Barra, whose commentary was hijacked at half time by an IRA man in 1933; the chairman of the Munster Council, Father Michael Hamilton, who had given the wrong score at the end of the 1937 all-Ireland football final; and, after Tomás Ó Laoi and Dave Hanley were briefly trialled, the youthful Mícheál O'Hehir, who had filled the role with aplomb from 1938 until, and indeed after, the advent of television in 1961. With Ó Muircheartaigh the tradition was in safe hands.

Television was another story. Ireland had delayed the introduction of its own television station for ten years to 1961 (one Government minister described television in 1956 as a luxury we could do well without) and has suffered since by comparison with the better-resourced English equivalent, to which the east coast and much of the north-west had access.

Dubliners in the 1970s were watching 'Match of the Day' rather than the 'Late Late Show', and RTE's attempts to compete were anaemic. The purchase of a three-camera video unit in 1976 improved things slightly. Mick Dunne put together a preview programme, broadcast during the Saturday afternoon sports programme, and the 'Sunday Game' review programme was introduced in 1979, showing highlights from the day's main GAA matches.

It was an uncertain start. Technical production, commentary and analysis were all found wanting in comparison with English soccer coverage.

The BBC is inflicting a Gaelic culture on Protestants, and Protestants are becoming increasingly resentful.
—COUNCILLOR DANNY KENNEDY, UUP, September 1991

The GAA knew it wasn't getting the service it deserved. It just didn't know what it was it deserved. The answer came in 1990 from an unlikely quarter: the BBC.

The BBC in Northern Ireland had determinedly ignored Gaelic games through much of its history. When sports results were first broadcast by the station in 1934, its director, George Marshall, ruled that GAA results be excluded on the grounds that they were 'hurting the feelings of the large majority of people in Northern Ireland.' In 1952 the station was given instructions from England to carry GAA results, but it still refused to do so on the grounds that the matches were played on Sundays, and results couldn't be carried on the Sabbath. It was 1966 before GAA results were covered by the station, and as late as 1984 Down County Board presented a media survey to the BBC contrasting the coverage of minor sports, such as cricket and hockey, with the minuscule level of GAA coverage.

Then, in 1990, the Ulster Council sold the rights to the

Ulster Championship to the BBC. Football followers got their first glimpse of high-quality coverage. The BBC arrived with eight cameras at a first round championship match. RTE only ever brought four at the most. For the 1990 Ulster final the BBC had seventeen cameras, more than had ever been present at a GAA match. The BBC coverage was more pacey, their presenters more relaxed. Their commentators, Jimmy Smyth and Peter McGinnity, proved knowledgeable and media-savvy and offered more thoughtful overviews of the games. They introduced an audience-participation angle.

Cameras were placed at the back of the net, and aerial views were able to run replays of off-the-ball incidents. The GAA wanted to know why RTE couldn't do the same.

The negotiations with RTE's head of sport, Tim O'Connor, were usually tense and fractious. O'Connor had seen the trend throughout Europe towards more live sport. The tradition of RTE coverage since 1962 had been to offer live coverage of the Railway Cup finals, all-Ireland semi-finals and finals and nothing more. This had been extended in 1989 to the Munster hurling final, the first provincial championship match to be televised live by RTE. Viewing figures were good. With the English soccer league now freeing up the terms of its own live television rights, O'Connor was interested in more live coverage but, hamstrung by RTE budgets, not in the associated costs.

Relations between the GAA and RTE reached a nadir in 1990 with the international-rules series between Ireland and Australia. RTE showed only edited highlights of two of the Australian rules tests and lost the tape of another. In the words of Clíona Foley, 'The grassroots tore themselves up from the ditches (from which they so often hurl) and revolted.'

Motions of condemnation were passed at county conventions and the national congress. RTE responded by extending its Sunday highlights programme during the summer of 1991 to show what they called '50 per cent more action.' The length of the programme was increased from sixty to ninety minutes.

O'Connor used the 1991 matches to establish the principle of live-television GAA matches. The fourth match of the series was the first GAA match broadcast live on a Saturday. It attracted 611,000 viewers, 40,000 more than the Rugby World Cup quarter final between Ireland and Australia, and it was the second most viewed football match after the 749,000 who watched the all-Ireland final.

———

We intend to use sports as a battering-ram and a lead offering in all our pay-television operations.
—RUPERT MURDOCH, message to shareholders, 1996

While the GAA and RTE were sorting out the nuances of live television, one of the world's most adventurous television entrepreneurs was facing bankruptcy. In a room in New York, Rupert Murdoch was signing a deal that would eradicate local sports everywhere, consigning them to the margins of history, the subject matter for folksy nostalgia.

Satellite television's first faltering steps almost bankrupted Murdoch. He launched Sky Television in February 1989 with four channels, a potential audience of 600,000 and a shortage of satellite dishes.

Two months later British Satellite Broadcasting (BSB) launched with five channels and a shortage of their distinctive 'squarial' antennae. The stations merged in November 1990 to form BSkyB after a ruinous fight for viewers, which cost £1¼ billion. The squarial was abandoned, and there were wholesale redundancies among BSB's 560 employees. Murdoch, straining under the debts accumulated by Sky, his attempt to transform a gaggle of local television stations in America into a national network and his invasion of satellite broadcasting in Britain, was saved by a Brazilian-style rescue by his banks. Near-bankruptcy left him chastened. But he had a plan. There was something beyond 'The Simpsons' and 'Beverly Hills, 90210': Americans had paid $35 to watch Mike Tyson box Donovan Ruddock.

The BSkyB sports desk wound down its operations on 20 January 1991. The few—too few—viewers it had accumulated mourned the demise of an adventurous half-hourly sports bulletin. The range on offer, to modern viewers, was weak. To Sky's eclectic sports mix of world-title fights, cricket from Australia, jumbo truck-racing from places nobody had heard of and obscure water sports, came a new merged sports set-up of soccer from Scotland and England's FA Cups, Italy's league, rugby league from England and Australian Open tennis.

In May 1991 BSkyB re-emerged with a £200 million war chest. A £304 million deal with the the Football Association, the English soccer body, was signed. In February 1993 BSkyB reported its first profit of £7½ million.

Murdoch was changing the environment in which sports operated much more quickly than most people realised. The sports authorities were delighted to be liberated from their dependence on terrestrial television and its low yields. They readily changed the timing of important matches to Sunday afternoons and Monday nights.

Murdoch talked about how television had liberated people from the once-powerful media barons. He meant the exact opposite: television had been liberated from regulation. It was more in the hands of media barons than ever.

To sports like soccer, Sky's sudden growth in the two years 1991–3 brought the promise of untold wealth. To sports like rugby league it brought the illusion of financial success, but it ultimately damaged their profile.

And for sports like Gaelic football it forced them to rethink their relationship with television. Television was, for the first time, a potential source of income.

―――

It could be altitude or tiredness or a combination of both. It's hard to tell.
—CIARÁN FITZGERALD, manager of the Irish rugby team, after Ireland's shock 15-6 defeat by Namibia, 20 July 1991

Luckily for the GAA the competition from other sports wasn't overwhelming. Irish rugby had briefly celebrated limited success at the start of the 1980s and was deprived of a World Cup semi-final place the October after Deadlock by a famous last-minute try by Australia's Michael Lynagh.

Otherwise it was a lost decade for the national team, which was running up a record-breaking collection of wooden spoons and second-last finishes. Between 1987 and 1998 Ireland was never out of the bottom two in the Five Nations Championship. They even managed to lose to Namibia twice in 1991 in tour warm-up test matches, an experience the eloquent second-row Neil Francis afterwards referred to as 'my tour in Nam.' They lost to Gloucester in another 1991 World Cup warm-up match, conceded a record eleven tries against the All Blacks in 1992 and became the first of the 'elite' top-eight countries to lose to Italy in 1995. The jokers were back in 1996 when Ireland lost a tour match in Lansdowne Road to Western Samoa: 'What would have happened if we had played the *whole* of Samoa.'

It was with justified trepidation that the pipe-smoking gentlemen who ran Irish rugby contemplated the move to professionalism in 1995. Ireland were at the bottom rank in a game played seriously by only ten countries.

──────

What chance had Ireland when we spent just £2 million on our athletes over the past four years.

—The Minister for Sport, FRANK FAHEY, reacts to Ireland's performances at the Seoul Olympics, 29 October 1988

The Irish sporting under-achievement of the decade came on an even bigger stage. Ireland usually aspires to, at best, a top-forty place in the Summer Olympics medals table—an under-performance in itself. But 1988 was a spectacular failure.

Ireland sent its largest representation ever, sixty-one athletes, to the Seoul Summer Olympics in 1988 and failed to get a top-ten finish from any of them, unless you count two hockey players on the British team who won 0.18 per cent of a silver medal between them.

It was our worst Olympic performance by a Soviet javelin throw, and, despite the bleatings of the Olympic Council of Ireland's self-important blazer-bearing officials, it couldn't be blamed on Ireland's small size.

Of countries with smaller populations, New Zealand won three gold, two silver and eight bronze medals. Norway won two gold and three silver, and Finland won a gold, a silver and two bronze.

There have been more hopelessly inept incidents in Irish Olympic history. Chief among them are the 4 × 100 freestyle swimming relay team of 1972 of Anne O'Connor, Christine Fulcher, Brenda McGrory and Aisling O'Leary, who had a length of the pool still to complete when East Germany won the gold medal; the RUC man Ken Stanford, who found that his pistol jammed and had to carry out emergency repairs in mid-competition in 1980; the modern pentathlete Sackville Currie, who managed to incur a world record of 2,000 penalty points by jumping the equestrian course backwards at the Moscow Olympics; and the hammer-thrower Declan Hegarty, who released his hammer at the wrong point three times in succession in Los Angeles in 1984 and demolished the protective netting.

The spectacular lack of success at Seoul hadn't even got the compensation of such amusement, or indeed of the medal-depriving disqualification and humiliation later provided by Cian O'Connor's substance-laden horse.

The celebrated victories of Eamonn Coghlan in the 1983 world championship 5,000 metres, of Barry McGuigan in beating Eusebio Pedroza for the lesser version of the world featherweight title in 1985, of Stephen Roche's Tour de France win in 1987 and of Dennis Taylor's world title in the distinctively minority sport of snooker in 1985 all proved to be one-off victories, worthy of a bus-top parade through Dublin but not enough to have an impact on Ireland's general sporting ineptitude. Indeed, Coghlan's tenure as chief executive of the turbulent Athletics Association of Ireland was coming to an end just as Deadlock fever was beginning to grip the country.

As a result of some sordid squabbles at the beginning of the twentieth century, soccer held a special revulsion for some GAA officials—a revulsion reciprocated by some soccer officials and fans.

By the summer of 1990 some of association football's loudest cheerleaders were rejoicing at the long-awaited prospect of soccer occupying the GAA's historic place at the heart of Irish sporting culture.

Forty years ago players did not train as hard or as often as they do today. We did not have a television station and the media hype was not as pronounced as it is today. Furthermore 13 of the present Meath panel are married in comparison with one of the 1949 team. So the sacrifices and tensions involved are not confined to individuals and in many cases [extend] to wives and families.

—FRANKIE BYRNE, star of Meath's three-times encounter with Louth in 1949, letter to the *Irish Times*, 3 July 1991

The GAA in 1991 didn't regard the past as anything like a Hartleyesque foreign country. It celebrated the past as enthusiastically as the future. The first question about any proposed change before the annual congress was how it would relate to the tradition of the game. The past *was* its future.

The organisation was in thrall to its magnificent history, its dominance of sport and its central place in popular culture.

You could see why. The GAA was good at history. Its growth was extraordinary, from 217 clubs in 1895 (when all other sporting organisations had a total of 120 affiliated clubs between them) to 360 in 1897, 768 in 1907, 1,000 in 1924, 1,686 in 1935, 2,010 in 1945, 2,226 in 1950 and 2,850 in 1960. In the 1920s it had overtaken rugby and soccer as the most popular spectator sport. All-Ireland final attendance broke through the 40,000 mark in 1929 to peak at 90,000 in 1961. In 1991 it had 750,00 paid-up members and 306,000 playing members over the age of fourteen. It was generating an income of £6 million between the Central Council and four provincial councils—more finance than its rivals the Rugby Union, two soccer associations and the mix of seventy-one other sports bodies trying to operate what passed for an Irish sporting movement.

This success was the argument that the GAA used when it

faced its critics, those who regarded the organisation as hidebound by ideology and rooted in an outdated, rural mindset. Any compromise would mean endangering the decades of growth built on the hard work of generations of committed, unpaid and ideologically motivated volunteers.

By 1991 there was a new critique emerging, both external and internal, which accused the GAA of not being inclusive, modernist or active enough for the changing times. The new President of Ireland, Mary Robinson, who Fintan O'Toole described as 'the living embodiment of all the social forces that are undermining the great Irish Ireland traditions of the association', saw fit to lecture the GAA on its requirement 'to embrace, openly and positively, new ideas and cultures.'

It was often said—most famously by the Minister for Finance and later EU commissioner, Charlie McCreevy—that the GAA, the Catholic Church and Fianna Fáil were the bulwarks of rural Ireland. That this was unfair and trite was already clear by the year of Deadlock. The GAA was as strong as ever, while the other 'bulwarks' were rapidly losing ground: Fianna Fáil had fallen from the level of 42 per cent, which it had enjoyed until the 1980s, down to 30 per cent (or even lower in some opinion polls); and church attendance (all churches) had fallen from the 1960s level of 80 per cent and higher down to 30 per cent or lower.

With the exception of Derry, the GAA was as strong in the cities as in any rural area, although a Dublin revival in 1974 had a bigger effect on spectator allegiance than on the participatory base.

Nine years earlier the GAA had spent an entire year celebrating its history as part of its centenary year. Breandán Ó hEithir's seminal description of the GAA in this year in *Over the Bar: A Personal Relationship with the GAA* (1984) showed that GAA history was different things to different people. In many ways, that had been the secret of its success.

But the formula was now under threat. Events of the 1980s showed that Irish sports fans were more willing than their parents to change their allegiance among the three major team sports.

———

The tension is not just on the day. With this particular fixture this tension and hype began to build on the day the draw was made.

—TERRY FERGUSON

Like all bureaucrats, GAA bureaucrats love planning. They like predictability, and two provincial councils, Leinster and Munster, had seeded their draws for the championship, effectually limiting the options for the final to two teams in the case of Leinster hurling and Munster football, or four in the case of Leinster football and Munster hurling.

The practice of seeding was unchallenged. All but a few inconsequential and weak counties thought it A Good Thing. It added another grey stone or two to the ancient, intricate web of walls known as the all-Ireland championship.

This was a pity: when seeding ended it had been good for the game. Leinster decided to stop seeding the hurling finalists in 1980, enabling Offaly to make a surprise breakthrough and win the Leinster championship and a surprise all-Ireland championship the following year. Ten years later they decided to put an end to the practice, instituted in 1962, of seeding the previous year's semi-finalists in four quarter-finals.

Munster had kept Cork and Kerry apart in their football semi-finals until 1992, when a change to the system enabled Clare to make a similar surprise breakthrough.

The draws for the four provincial championships of 1991

were low-profile affairs. It wasn't the practice of the press to cover the draws. Even if they wanted to, the press was excluded from Leinster Council meetings at the time and was left waiting outside in the rain for a *'habeas combatus'* sheet of paper to be delivered at the end of the meeting, as happened in Tullamore in 1982.

The momentous Leinster Council meeting at Portlaoise on 8 August 1990, which drew Meath and Dublin in the first round of the championship, had begun with a debate in another direction, that of dividing the championship on a north-south basis. Jimmy Gray of Dublin, the council chairman, asked for any contributions from the floor. Kildare proposed the open draw, Offaly seconded, and it was voted through.

Then came the relatively unsophisticated process of the draw itself, made by means of table-tennis balls (with names attached) drawn from a bag.

The draw wasn't reported for a number of days. The Leinster Council secretary, Michael Delaney, mentioned it in conversation to Seán McGoldrick, then of the *Irish Press*. The news spread. Far from being regarded as an enlightened decision, one that would change the GAA and the shape of an Irish summer, the reaction was overwhelmingly critical.

'In the past the Leinster Council has shown itself to be one of the more sensible of the many units which make up the GAA,' the *Irish Independent* GAA correspondent Donal Keenan wrote.

That reputation was badly tarnished. Democracy went crazy when it was decided to hold an open-draw championship without seeding at least the two finalists from this year. The delegates from the weaker counties seized on the opportunity to enhance their chances of reaching a Leinster final without considering the real impact this would have on Leinster football and the game in general.

Colm O'Rourke described it as lunacy: 'This change has destroyed the Leinster final, the game with most appeal in all of Ireland over several years.'

'How anyone could allow Meath and Dublin to be drawn together in the first round of the championship is beyond belief,' Gerry Hargan said. David Beggy commented:

> It seems the height of madness. It just doesn't make sense. What is the reason for this? Is it to make it easier for weaker counties to reach the Leinster final? If that is the reason then it is totally ridiculous. If they think this is going to improve the game they are making a mistake with the standard that is there at the moment.

Michael Delaney was worried about the financial implications. But he replied to newspaper queries and was optimistic that Meath v. Dublin would attract a crowd of 35,000.

Would they what! The following year's draws were made live on RTE radio. Subsequently the championship draw developed into a television event. The days of pulling labelled tennis balls out of a bowl behind closed doors were over.

| ITALIA '90

I missed Italia '90 because I was at the World Cup.

—CON HOULIHAN

I f you looked closely at the banners that Offaly supporters brought to the 1981 and 1982 all-Ireland finals, ten years before Deadlock, who could have seen that the supporters were not as particular as a previous generation had been?

Offaly tricolours easily double as Irish tricolours, and, as well as the usual collection of weak puns ('Furlong Rhode a Darby Winner'), there were several whose slogans ignored Offaly, instead extolling the Irish soccer team's anticipated heroism in coming matches against the Dutch in Rotterdam—two particularly tidy operations that resulted in a draw and an unlucky defeat. These were the fans of the new age, multi-cultural and bemused by any name-calling between the rival sports of Ireland.

There shouldn't have been so much surprise at this or at the 'Hill 16 on tour' banners that were making their appearances wherever Ireland played. Soccer in Ireland had a laudable history for decades before the arrival of a Yorkshire fishing enthusiast as national team manager in 1986.

The problem was that much of it seemed a long time ago. At the time, England dominated the world game, and the Four Nations Championship served as an effectual World

Cup (Ireland had won the competition in 1914). A team that straddled the political divide of the Civil War as effectively as the GAA—and even more effectively straddled the cross-religious divide—had gone to the quarter-finals of the Olympics in 1924.

The North, with several part-timers and a sabbatarian who refused to play on Sundays in their squad, reached the quarter-finals of the 1958 World Cup. Ireland were back in the last eight of the European Championship in 1962, almost beating Austria to reach the semi-finals. The North went to the World Cup in 1982, reaching the last twelve, and in 1986, reaching the last sixteen, while the Football Association of Ireland had notched up victories over most of the leading soccer-playing nations in the 1980s, including Brazil, and had come within goal difference of qualification from one of the toughest World Cup qualifying groups in 1982.

The GAA had viewed the growth of support for soccer with confident indifference. Asked if they would change the starting times for the 1988 European Championship or 1990 World Cups, for which Ireland had qualified, the Ulster Council in particular had shown a determined indifference.

Others were not so sure. Soccer summers were attaining a momentum of their own. These had more to do with the celebration of the new than anything that was happening on the distant fields of Gelsenkirchen and Genoa. When Christy Moore needed a ballad to represent 1980s urban Ireland he chose the story of Joxer and his journey to Stuttgart in 1988.

Soccer summers were beginning to resemble a pattern familiar to GAA aficionados: the GAA fanfare events of previous decades. The sporting dominance of the GAA had been founded on carnivals, initially on the deadlock of the football finals of 1903 or the hurling finals of 1931, and was sustained by the publicity coup of the Polo Grounds final of 1947, the Dublin-Kerry rivalry of the 1970s and the tragedy and romantic triumph of Kerry's failed five-in-a-row of 1982.

Euro '88, a week of unexpected success in the major tournament in which Ireland has come closest to winning to this day, hadn't dented the GAA's dominance. But Italia '90 proved to be a different matter.

——

It was an expensive lesson to us not to put fixtures up against televised sporting events where the Irish team are playing.

—MICHAEL DELANEY, report to Leinster Convention,
February 1991

The 1990 Leinster championship in particular was overshadowed by Italia '90. The Leinster hurling semi-finals were played in mid-June. It had become a very attractive date on the calendar, thanks to the rise of Offaly hurling a decade before Deadlock, and, to a lesser extent, to Laois hurling and, later, to Dublin hurling. In 1984 the attendance at the Leinster hurling semi-finals—33,061—exceeded that at the final between Offaly and Wexford   30,016   for the first time in history,

This situation was repeated twice in three years: in 1987, when the attendance was 35,719 at the semi-finals and 29,133 at the final; and 1989, when 33,512 attended the semi-finals and 24,519 attended the final, which was between Offaly and Kilkenny in both years.

In 1990 it was a different story, and the vulnerability of the structure was evident. The Leinster hurling semi-finals clashed with an Ireland-Egypt soccer game on a Sunday afternoon, and the attendance halved, to 17,436. The attendance was only part of the story, as many of the crowd left the stadium as soon as the first semi-final was over to watch the soccer on television. The Leinster secretary, Michael Delaney, told an anniversary documentary about the Deadlock series that 'we had less than 10,000 people at the game—maybe an awful lot less.' In 1991, by comparison, the attendance at the Leinster hurling semi-final was back up to 31,653.

Two weeks later Meath qualified to play Laois in a Leinster football semi-final the day after 'Totò' Schillaci's goal had sent Ireland packing from the World Cup. When Jack Charlton and the soccer team arrived at the airport on the Sunday afternoon, a quarter of a million people turned up to greet them. More people showed up to welcome them home than welcomed home the winning German team with the World Cup a week later.

In Croke Park the attendance at the football was 11,682. 'We took a financial hit,' Delaney said.

Attendances everywhere were down, even at those matches that didn't clash with Italia '90. The Dublin-Wicklow semi-final at Droichead Nua attracted just 8,000 people, the sort of figure that could be anticipated at a Kildare county final between two reasonably supported clubs. Laois-Offaly in Croke Park, two days after Ireland's draw with England, attracted just 10,000.

The Leinster Council was in trouble. Their operating surplus to November 1990 showed a decline of £158,000, down 70 per cent on 1989. The 1989 championship takings, £610,718, were down to £472,726, with gate receipts at the hurling semi-finals alone down from £102,040 to £46,020. Many of the council delegates agreed afterwards that it was a mistake not to avoid a clash with the televised World Cup game. Another problem was that Dublin and Offaly qualified for the Leinster hurling final, for which receipts were down by £12,000. The council had to take the decision in January 1991 to cut back drastically on expenditure on county grounds within the province. They had already anticipated expenditure of £150,000 on promoting and developing the games in primary schools.

Delaney has said that the only thing that saved his council was the Dublin-Meath Deadlock series in 1991. In fact the Dublin-Meath rivalry was already bailing the council out: it drew 53,847 people to the final four weeks after Ireland's exit from Italia '90, bringing in more than half the council's income for the year.

The council had just agreed to purchase new buildings for its headquarters that summer of 1991. Delaney said to his chairman, Jack Boothman, 'I think we may talk to an auctioneer. We won't be able to sustain this building here.'

Delaney wasn't alone. The attendance at the Ulster final was down 10,000 to 20,000, and Donegal v. Derry, which clashed with Ireland v. Egypt, was down to 6,000, reflecting the historically high level of interest in soccer in the north-west.

Attendances held up better in other provinces. On the day the homecoming from Italia '90 was televised, 40,065 people came out to see the Munster final between Cork and Kerry— 7,000 down on 1989 but by no means in the penury department. The Connacht final attendance was 18,000, just 2,000 down on 1989.

The hit taken by Leinster, and the perception created by blanket media coverage, had more impact than the cold statistics of the turnstiles. 'Italia '90,' in the words of Bernard Flynn, 'had brainwashed the country. The GAA people had gone over to soccer.' An *Irish Independent* editorial opined that

> you can't but feel a little sympathy for the GAA . . . But then, perhaps, if the GAA got its act together, like introducing the Open Draw, establishing a discernible

and enforceable set of rules for its football games, properly train its referees and stick rigidly to a stiff set of penalties for players who bring its games into disrepute, it wouldn't have to be continually looking over its shoulder at soccer.

————

This was not like Italia '90 at all. Where was the sunshine, the spaghetti, the wine?
> —NELL MCCAFFERTY compares Dublin-Meath 1991 with Italia '90

Some of the media coverage of the events of 1988 and 1990 seemed to indicate that soccer was now becoming the mainstream sport and that Gaelic football was being confined to the margins.

The GAA bridled at such suggestions but decided to keep its dignity and its distance as it watched a collection of vested interests ramping up the significance of the Charlton team's achievement. Irish sport, we were told, was transformed forever. One edition of the RTE radio programme 'What If' ascribed to the excitement of Italia '90 the origins of the boom years, which were dubbed 'the Celtic Tiger' by the economist Kevin Gardner as early as 1994. The liberation of women in sport, the reclaiming of the tricolour from Northern Ireland extremists and the unleashing of a barstool sports culture were all attributed to Italia '90 with confidence by later commentators.

In the circumstances, the coverage could turn nasty. References to Gaelic football as 'bogball' and hurling as 'stick-fighting', borrowed from Northern Ireland's sectarian lexicon, were used by such critics as Declan Lynch of the *Sunday Independent*.

Such vulgarity wasn't confined to the lunatic fringes of the supporters. One FAI council member reacted to the news that Croke Park was to be developed by the GAA by saying that it would bankrupt the association: 'We'll get Croke Park, and the muck savages will be back togging out in the ditch.'

Declan Lynch was on the way to becoming the decade's most talented controversialist through his columns in *Hot Press*, the *Irish Press* and later the *Sunday Independent*. He would write the best reminiscence on Italia '90 as an event rather than as a sporting contest. But that was in the future.

Away from the knockabout inhabited by Lynch and his colleague and friend George Byrne, there was a more serious debate. The editorial opinions of the leading Dublin newspapers were critical of the GAA for its failure to accommodate the rival sports—usually, but not always, soccer. The influential *Irish Times* columnist Fintan O'Toole described the GAA as 'terrified to face the sectarian and bigoted elements within its own identity' and as taking 'refuge in a fog of official-speak.'

There was a broadside from another interested party who was at the tail end of an even more controversial career. The debate was ignited during the 1988 European Championship by Conor Cruise O'Brien, one of the first Irish politicians to question the national consensus on reunification, and later a leading Unionist politician in his own right. O'Brien was a prolific columnist in several newspapers, and his contributions to the *London Times* during the championship set out the terms of a new debate between GAA and soccer.

Initially it followed a familiar line on the contrast between the behaviour of Irish and English soccer supporters (a far more complex question than his article, and many others on the subject, could hope to explain).

One of the biggest English stereotypes of the Irish is that they are especially given to drunken brawls. But in West Germany it was the English who were the drunken brawlers, while the Irish were behaving with [the] civility and restraint which the English like to ascribe to themselves.

So far so good. But his next passage claimed that the Irish fans were well behaved for the sole reason that they didn't include GAA supporters.

Pent up fury goes into political nationalism . . . Soccer in the Irish republic is not a nationalist game. IRA sympathisers support Gaelic games and regard soccer as a foreign game.

O'Brien's article followed a pattern that had been established in the preceding weeks. The *Daily Mail*, previewing Euro '88 in the same vein, remarked that 'no GAA match is complete without a fight among the spectators.'

One writer who rushed to defend the association was the *Irish Times* journalist Seán Kilfeather, who was described at his funeral by one orator as the embodiment of 'righteous indignation'. Kilfeather pointed out that GAA fans never needed to be segregated, while soccer fans always were.

The GAA's official reply wasn't as coherent as it might have been. Much of it was left in the hands of Danny Lynch, the spokesman who was wheeled out to defend the increasingly petulant decisions of the central body. Adept in a crisis, Lynch was less dexterous in cross-cultural debate. He was well regarded by the GAA-focused media, which he attempted to control with a mixture of bluster and humour.

Lynch, sent to bat for the GAA, replied that 'the good doctor has lost any meaningful understanding of what exactly occurs in Ireland.'

O'Brien wrote a series of letters to the newspapers answering his critics that they had seen the GAA version of his article, not the original. His case wasn't helped by the fact this was only the latest in a series of attacks on the GAA and its followers that he'd launched. No-one doubted that the affront was intentional, as was the inference that GAA fans were the moral equivalent of England's football hooligans, with soccer fans placed at a level above them. It was a deserved acknowledgement of the humour and decorum of the Irish soccer fan but an undeserved and outrageous affront to the GAA fan.

What O'Brien, and indeed many who entered the debate on both sides, didn't realise was that the two species had become virtually indistinguishable, and sports fans were equally at home at Cheltenham Racecourse, Twickenham, Estádio da Luz and Cusack Park in Mullingar, or at any other sports event where green was worn.

The spirit extended to the GAA's critics. O'Brien had lauded the GAA in the 1950s as a fine example of Irish community spirit. Declan Lynch had won an all-Ireland medal for Westmeath in a Scór quiz competition— something that was to enable him to gain admission to GAA club functions in his teenage years.

————

The figures being spoken in terms of monetary gain from these three games grew ever more astronomical. It made the FAI's little pile from the world cup look even more derisory.
            —TOM HUMPHRIES, after the third match of Deadlock

Soccer's journey to the promised land, to the heart of

popular culture in Ireland, would have to overcome a few unexpected and self-inflicted obstacles. In these years the beautiful game wasn't at its most attractive.

Italia '90 was a dismal World Cup. Jack Charlton's Irish team won a reputation for resilience rather than refinement, playing out a succession of draws that earned the continued enmity of many soccer lovers, not least the later FIFA president Sepp Blatter, whose memory of Italia '90 may have influenced his tendency to punctuate his term with Hibernophobic outbursts.

Italia '90 was as much about draws as the 1991 Deadlock would be, and as such it might have served as a dress rehearsal for the coming June and July—an Italia '91. The draws seemed to go on without end. In the last nine competitive soccer matches before Deadlock, Ireland had won one, lost one and drawn seven.

Although public interest remained high, the 1991 match against England in Wembley attracted a viewership of 1,307,000, an audience equal to that achieved in the World Cup finals. The series of draws said a lot about the limits of Irish ambition.

We were not confident enough to actually win anything— to go the whole way, as Denmark did at Euro '92—only to perform and not be beaten. 'You'll never beat the Irish,' they chanted on the terraces. 'Put them under pressure,' Charlton said in the phrase that became the theme song of the summer of 1990. 'Go and compete.' The chorus of the song filched from the Scottish team of 1978 said something about winning the World Cup—but nobody was ready to believe that.

————

Nobody demurred. Draws were, after all, an improvement. Ireland went five whole years without winning a single match between 1967 and 1971. What passed for the soccer aspirations of a previous generation was a series of 'moral victories'—such as losing 2-1 to Italy in 1972—that became the subject of a Dermot Morgan sketch. There was the feeling of being hard done by that resulted from refereeing decisions in Brussels, Paris and Sofia. Irish fans put up with them. They were not enough to satisfy the quest for celebration.

Nor were they the full story. When the pattern of draws changed, with Ireland's six wins in successive qualification matches before Italia '90 and three before Euro '88, so did the level of excitement and anticipation surrounding the team. Even the draws didn't matter any more as the mythology of Italia '90 was constructed—especially the penalty shoot-out after one of those dull draws, with Romania. Charlton subsequently eked out four successive wins leading up to USA '94, followed by a home defeat and a famous draw in Windsor Park and three wins at the start of the Euro '96 campaign. They will never be as widely remembered or commemorated as the draws. Mick McCarthy notched up two series of four wins in the qualification for World Cup 2002. Steve Staunton had four successive wins leading up to Euro 2008. All were quickly forgotten in soccer's selective memory.

Ireland never subsequently won six successive qualification matches under any manager other than Charlton—this despite the criticism levelled at Jack's style of football, and despite an opinion, placed almost as a matter of consensus, by the force of the personality of the television pundit, and Charlton's harshest critic, Eamon Dunphy. Dunphy, who, it's sometimes forgotten, was also one of the country's most highly qualified coaches, was appointed as FAI youth manager and was sacked almost immediately for criticising his bosses in his column in the *Sunday Tribune*. 'There is a substantial gap between the glory of civic receptions and reality, the reality of professional soccer,'

Dunphy wrote as early as 1988. 'Somewhere in between the two, the reality of Irish soccer must lie.'

Nor was the FAI clear-headed in its reaction to its new-found success and wealth. The players seized on the inexperience of the soccer officials and took the opportunity to negotiate an avaricious deal for their participation in the finals, earning more per player than the German team that won the championship.

The largesse that went to the FAI might have been used to lift the game out of its organisational and financial morass. 'I would be worried if the Rugby Union got a big cash injection like that,' the incoming Leinster GAA chairman, Jack Boothman, said; 'but not the soccer association.' His insight was derived from history. When asked if he would become secretary of the FAI in the 1950s, the athletics promoter Billy Morton responded: 'Too many of those fellows have their bicycles chained to the railings.' He was referring to the lack of vision and ambition of those who ran soccer from its Merrion Square headquarters.

Soccer, which had six major stadiums in Dublin in the 1930s—when the GAA had one—had two by 1990. One of the iconic Dublin venues, Glenmalure Park in Milltown, acquired from the Jesuits in the 1920s on the understanding that it would remain a sports ground in perpetuity, had been sold off for private gain as a housing estate in the 1980s. In Cork, Flower Lodge was sold to the GAA to become Páirc Uí Rinn.

Two of the longest-standing soccer clubs, Shelbourne and Shamrock Rovers, were homeless. The average attendance in the League of Ireland premier division, a competition that still struggled to create any level of interest through the most dismal months, were up 20 per cent in the season after Italia '90, and the league had its largest crowd for years at St Patrick's Athletic v. Cork City in Harold's Cross. Attendances still hovered around 1,200.

While the game's officials and its elite clubs were mired in panicked inaction, the Italia '90 revolution was transforming the grass roots of the game despite its organisational defects and with precious little help from the Merrion Square headquarters. An Irish soccer census in December 1991 plotted the impact of Italia '90: the sport now had more clubs than the GAA, with 3,247, although fewer teams, at 7,983 (38 senior, 119 intermediate, 2,358 junior, 436 youth, 2,622 schoolboys, 664 schools, 324 others). The sport had 142,009 registered players, and the association calculated that 250,000 people were actively involved in playing and administering Irish soccer every weekend from August to June each season.

While infrastructure remained a problem, a start was made with the help of World Cup money. The FAI developed county grounds to act as focus points for their growing network of leagues in rural areas, many in traditional Gaelic heartlands. One of the first was in Navan.

———

Dublin versus Meath is a real derby. What does United versus City mean to Ronaldo or Sibierski?

—TOM HUMPHRIES

None of the officials at the 1991 GAA congress in the Burlington Hotel would admit it, but there was one dramatic effect from Italia '90 that was to influence the association. Weaker counties had been inspired by the fact that the FAI had used the parentage and grand-parentage rules to increase its playing strength. The ruse wasn't new. Shay Brennan, though born in Manchester, had played for Ireland on parentage grounds as early as 1964.

After 1979, when entitlement to an Irish passport became the sole requirement, the FAI actively set out to expand its selection pool by recruiting English players of Irish parentage. The name of the FAI was wittily ascribed to 'Find an Irishman', and the situation became absurd in 1980 with the case of Michael Robinson, whose great-grandmother Eliza Morgan was from Cork. Robinson was able to play for Ireland as a result of his mother taking out Irish citizenship. (This situation was repeated in 1992 with Tommy Coyne.) The declarations of Alan Kernaghan in 1992, whose parents came from Bangor, of Jason McAteer in 1994, whose grandfather came from Co. Down, and James Quigley, a youth international from Derry with no obvious credentials on the other side of the border, who declared for the Republic under the passport rule, caused renewed controversy.

(Basketball too was to find Irishmen in the United States, notably Marty Conlon, born in New York, who played NBA basketball for the Milwaukee Bucks. Irish cricket found its own non-native Irishmen in South Africa, Australia and New Zealand, most notably Trent Johnston, the star of the 2008 World Cup victory over Pakistan.)

The significance of a parentage rule was soon realised by the GAA's smaller counties. The Central Council allowed the parentage rule to be extended to nominated 'weaker' counties. Jason Ward, the star of Leitrim's 1994 Connacht championship, and whose father, Des, came from Aughnasheelin, was the first beneficiary of the GAA's new parentage rule in January 1993, when he lined out against Fermanagh in a challenge.

The GAA has strenuously denied rumours of approaches for sponsorship by the National Lottery. We have draws every week.

—Joke current in June 1991

Italia '90, or rather the advertisements on soccer club jerseys, had shown the GAA that sponsorship mattered in modern sport. But it wasn't sure how it would work. Neither, for that matter, was the FAI, who ended up with Opel as sponsors solely because of a phone call to Arnold O'Byrne, looking for a raffle prize. Nor, indeed, was anyone else in Irish sport. But in 1991, just in time for the Deadlock series, the GAA legalised jersey sponsorship.

The GAA had no marketing strategy, no evaluation reports, no idea of exactly what it had to sell. Despite its enthusiastic endorsement, and a certain deal of commercial showboating after the motion was passed, it was too early to evaluate what the 1991 sponsorship motion meant.

One businessman was quoted in the newspapers as saying that he would sponsor an all-Ireland team for £2 million, before the ink was dry on the reports from the congress. It was clear that he was talking about Dublin, but it was a fiction: nobody was yet ready to commit a twentieth of that figure to sponsor a county team.

Oddly enough, at a time when sponsorship wasn't yet legal Dublin already had a sponsor: a much-publicised deal with Kaliber, of the Guinness Group. For £20,000 a year the Dublin players wore the Kaliber logo on their training tracksuits—but not in matches. Kaliber was delighted when Paddy Cullen was appointed manager of Dublin in 1980. With a publican at the helm, things couldn't get any better. They didn't. Then Dublin reached the national league final and allowed National Irish Bank to sponsor them for one match. Kaliber, and the giant group that marketed them, cut off their dealings with the Dublin County Board.

As a result, for the first of the four games Dublin had no logo on their shirts. Between the first and second matches of the series Con Clarke, the vice chairman, and Fintan Drury finalised a £50,000 two-year deal with the former Dublin

hurler Bill Kelly of Arnott's. Although a huge logo was put on
display, at a hastily organised press conference neither the
firm nor the county board were sure how the jerseys would
look a few days later. Things had moved on since Arnott's
had ruffled GAA officials by presenting Paddy Cullen and his
colleagues with a set of shirts in the 1970s.

For the second game Dublin had a very small crest from
Arnott's. For the third they had a very large logo across their
chest. The deal stuck. Arnott's remained Dublin's sponsors
for eighteen years, with Séamus Deignan continuing Kelly's
support and increasing their cover first to €300,000 and then
to €600,000 a year, until they were replaced by a six-year
€4.65 million deal with Vodafone in January 2010.

———

O'Reilly Transport at Dundalk and the Meath County
Board made an agreement that the company would
sponsor the Meath senior football team for the first
round of the Leinster championship. The agreement
includes all replays. Meath County Board have informed
the company of its intention not to honour this
agreement.

—Statement by O'REILLY TRANSPORT, 18 June 1991

Meath had sponsorship travails of their own. On the
Thursday before the first match, the county board reported
that O'Reilly Transport, from Newry, had done a deal with
Meath for £10,000 a year and that Meath would wear the logo
in the Dublin match on 2 June. The deal was for one match,
according to the county board. O'Reilly Transport issued a
statement saying that the deal applied to replays as well, and
the players wore the logo again for the second match.

But it was becoming increasingly clear that the manager,

Seán Boylan, and the county board were not in agreement. Boylan was upset that his old friend Noel Keating, from Co. Clare, had not been offered first option on the sponsorship. Keating had left Kilrush at sixteen to work in Dublin and opened a butcher's shop in Francis Street in the Liberties before establishing the Kepak beef plant in Clonee. His company had the distinction of introducing the 'quarter-pounder' beef burger to Ireland and well-known brands such as Big Al's and Rustlers. He was in expansion mode, having opened plants in Hacketstown, Athleague and Ballymahon, and he had an eye on the English retail trade. His friendship with Boylan led to his hosting the 1987 all-Ireland winning team for a stopover *en route* to Co. Meath, an event that turned into a barbecue for five thousand people.

Keating got involved in the squad preparations (sharing the Gormanston swimming pool with the players), and he went on the trip to the Buchanan Arms Hotel, in Drymen, between the third and fourth matches of the 1991 Deadlock and on the Florida holiday afterwards. Sadly, he collapsed and died at the age of fifty-three in 1993.

Kepak was contracted as the sponsor of Meath for one game, as O'Reilly Transport had been. That was all Keating needed to establish himself. He then agreed to match every pound raised by the county board. A hundred centimetres of real estate on the Meath jersey was worth £30,000 to Kepak; the same proportion of Dublin's jersey was worth £60,000 to Arnott's.

You could buy a house in Terenure for £60,000.

Chapter 3 ∾

| CHANGING GAME

A vital part of Gaelic football's greatness is the sheer scale of its physical demands. It demands greater motivation and courage than any other ball game we have known in this country.
—LIAM HAYES, January 1997

Gaelic football had inherited some seemingly insurmountable problems in the years leading up to the Deadlock series. In football, as in moral politics, the 1980s had been an angry decade. Many of the most significant matches were niggly and spiteful. Questions were being asked about the most basic aspects of the games. Man-to-man marking, the tackle, the shoulder charge and the disciplinary process were all under scrutiny.

The footballers of Dublin and Meath knew that only too well: they had precipitated much of the debate. The casualty list from the Dublin-Meath encounters of the 1980s would have filled a decent charge sheet at one of the courts where Tony Hanahoe's brother, and Tony himself, hoovered up legal-aid defence cases.

'The teams of the 1980s contained bigger and older players who could play the physical game to great advantage,' Eugene McGee commented. For Seán Boylan, 'to put it simply, games were more physical then.'

Actively maleficent might be a better description. Liam

Harnan had broken Barney Rock's collar bone in the league final of 1986; John Caffrey was sent off after an incident with Ben Tansey in 1984; Eamon Heery flattened Liam Hayes straight after the throw-in in 1987, a year in which Charlie Redmond and Kevin Foley were both sent off and twelve players were involved in various altercations; Dave Synnott was sent off in 1988 and Colm Coyle in 1989.

Various scorecards of real and imagined offences were also being recorded by individual players. Vinnie Murphy's punching of Kevin Foley, which led to Foley's sending off soon afterwards in the league final of 1988, was remembered and resented in Meath.

The day before the first match the up-and-coming bookmaker and publicity machine Paddy Power offered odds of 8-11 that one or more players would be sent off during seventy minutes of play, and he offered evens for all players to finish the match.

The crowds rejoiced in the prospect of an old-fashioned encounter that celebrated impulse and denigrated reason. As Colm O'Rourke wrote afterwards, 'the attendance proved something that people in high places do not like to admit publicly, the prospect of a row is a bigger attraction than high quality football.'

Paddy Power offered 11-1 the draw. Little did he know.

——

There was an awful lot of frees, but that was a time in Gaelic football that was nearly the norm, particularly matches between Dublin and Meath.

—CHARLIE REDMOND

The free-count for the four matches between Dublin and Meath in 1991 was indeed high—among the highest in championship history. Even under the new Hanahoe quick-restart rules they were too high to give the matches any credibility as spectacles: 65 in the second match (plus 25 in extra time), 48 in the third match (plus 19 in extra time), 48 in the fourth match and 47 in the first match. It puts the second match, the only match Meath dominated, among the most free-ridden matches in the history of the seventy-minute game, notably the shambolic 69-free all-Ireland final between Meath and Cork, while previous Meath-Cork encounters had produced 56 frees in 1988 and 51 in 1989, and the excessively physical Kerry-Roscommon final of 1980 had 64 frees. Previously the 1984 Leinster final between Dublin and Meath had 47 frees, and the 1986 final, when Meath made their breakthrough, had 33 in the second half.

The theory of the 1970s was that frees broke up the fluidity of a faster, fitter team. Two of Dublin's 1970s semi-finals were among the most free-ridden of all time: Dublin's 1975 semi-final against Galway had 67 and their 1975 semi-final against Derry had 66. The 1991 championship was particularly prone to frees: the referee, Denis Guerin, from Dublin, awarded 56 frees as Offaly beat Wexford, and there were 62 frees in the Connacht semi-final between Mayo and Galway. That theory hadn't entirely gone away in 1991.

The enhanced aggression of the games, which added so much to the appeal of a Dublin-Meath encounter, is easily explained. Gaelic football had a 78-year tradition of zonal systems and man-to-man marking, dating from the introduction of the fifteen-a-side game in 1913, which meant that opponents were facing the same player year after year.

To add to the problem, certain positions lent themselves to the picking of big muscular men, which meant that bigger, more muscular men had to be picked to mark them. Big often meant immobile; immobile often meant dirty.

Individual players faced a dilemma: even if your team

won, your opponent might humiliate you. All you had to do was bide your time and you would meet him again next year. A replay might give you an unexpected chance to restore your dignity. But four matches in six weeks? That had never happened before.

———

People should not be so naïve as not to understand that players who get knocked about may put in for it on occasions, by word or deed. There are unwritten codes in the game. One, for example, says that head-butting is a mortal sin. And if you head-butt someone then you take your medicine when it arrives.

—COLM O'ROURKE

The seemingly inflexible man-marking system left coaches with more options for innovation than might be expected. Over the decades, Dublin and Meath had been among the innovators who sought out alternative ways of playing the game.

The first and most unsophisticated subversion of the zonal system was the roaming full-forward, used by Dublin against Meath in 1955 to negate the presence of full-back Paddy 'Hands' O'Brien. This landmark encounter, which took place before most of the participants of Deadlock were born, was often used by Paddy Downey of the *Irish Times* and others to benchmark the subsequent rivalry between the teams.

A popular ploy of the 1970s and 80s was the third midfielder, as used initially by deep-lying half-forwards like Tyrone's Jack Teggart against Derry in 1957, Westmeath's Mick Carley against Dublin in 1962 and Dublin's Bill Casey against Kerry in 1965. Most famously, Meath used the corner-forward Ollie Shanley as a third midfielder in their 1967 all-Ireland final defeat of Cork.

Dublin used Casey again in November 1970 in a national league match against Offaly. (Dublin later used Shay Donnelly in the same role against Mayo in 1971.) Even the traditionalists, Kerry, used Séamus Fitzgerald in a league match against Offaly in 1969 and on several subsequent occasions.

The third midfielder was to become a common tactic after Dublin's John Caffrey was used there with great success in the 1983 championship. Mayo's Colm McMenamon filled the role in 1996, and Ger Brady of Ballina and Colm O'Neill of Crossmaglen Rangers both played third-midfielder roles in club finals. Boylan had Tommy Dowd as his third midfielder of choice.

One of the patterns of the 1991 series is that the traditional man-marking system broke down as games developed. Neither team was anxious to tinker with the system before the match, but by the end it was common for players to be out of position.

In the coming two decades more options were to arise, with Armagh and Tyrone preferring to place further players behind the ball and with Kerry sending the famous 'twin towers' into the front line; but, unlike the 2-3-5 system in soccer, the 3-3-2-3-3 system survived for a century after it was first devised in response to the reduction of teams to fifteen-a-side in 1913.

––––

The GAA now faces more competition from other sports. I am very confident that the new rules will make football far more attractive both for players and spectators. We will have a much better game and, as a result, greater attendances. A game that will stand up with the very best in the world.

—TONY HANAHOE in advance of the 1990 congress that introduced the free kick and sideline kick from the hands

Part of the problem with Gaelic football was that legislators were making up the rules as they went along. Half way through the 1982/3 league the personal foul was introduced. At a famous Railway Cup semi-final, John O'Keeffe, one of the cleanest players in the game, and one of the greatest full-backs of all time, was sent off by a perplexed Séamus Aldridge.

Seán Boylan points out somewhat triumphantly that Mick Lyons was sent off only twice in his career with Meath and that the first time it was for just such a personal foul, when Meath played Roscommon in Navan during that league series. The second time was in the 1991 Deadlock series.

The 1980s all-Irelands had been stop-start, foul-ridden affairs. Even more importantly, the first analysis in the history of the game showed that the ball was out of play more often than it was in play. For an astonishing nineteen minutes of each thirty minute period the ball was dead, waiting for kick-outs, frees or sideline balls to be taken. The ball was in play for only 37 per cent of the duration of an average Gaelic football match.

It wasn't the worst game for stoppages: an average NFL American football game has about six minutes of actual playing time per thirty minutes. On the other hand, even at the dullest of soccer World Cups, in 1990, the ball was in play on average for fifty-two minutes out of ninety (58 per cent)—although in some games it was as low as forty-five. And in rugby, in which there is an average of more than eighty stoppages a game, 'ball in play' time was 40–42 per cent, rising to 46 per cent, for the 2009 Super 14 tournament.

The 1990 congress was the first in five years that had the power to alter the rules of the game. It was surprisingly open to new ideas, and it ranks among the most liberal in GAA history.

This was important, because a specially convened rules-revision committee had placed three important rule changes on the agenda. Heavily influenced by Australian Rules, these were to transform the game of Gaelic football.

———

> If you look back at the games between Dublin and Kerry, the team that scored the first goal nearly always won. That was because they cut mistakes to a minimum. Yet the football was fast end-to-end stuff. I hope that we can see a return to that standard.
>
> —TONY HANAHOE, December 1990

Hanahoe's committee proposed five rule changes: the free kick and sideline kick from the hands were implemented; two that were not implemented were the kick out from the hands and the playing of the game over four quarters; and the handpass was redefined as 'releasing the ball with one or both hands, open or closed, provided there is a definitive striking action.'

When the new rules were introduced for the 1989/90 national league, the period the ball was in play for each thirty-minute period increased from eleven minutes to up to twenty-one minutes, under the four-quarter experimental rules—an unprecedented 70 per cent of playing time.

A survey by the Research and Statistics Department at Trinity College, Dublin, canvassed the opinions of players, officials and supporters. There was a 75 per cent increase in the number of goals scored, a 39 per cent increase in the number of points scored and a significant increase in the amount of uninterrupted play. Most importantly of all, the 'ball in play' times for an average match, even after the flow was interrupted by rule changes imposed by subsequent legislation, levelled out at 45 per cent, a figure comparable to rugby and soccer.

Hanahoe said that the new hand pass should be accepted because it gave the player in possession the opportunity of getting rid of the ball virtually at will.

The league had proved nothing: it would be in the white heat of the 1991 championship that the new code of rules would be tried and found to be adequate or not.

———

There was always a competitive streak in the matches between Dublin and Meath, and it got a bit nasty for a while. But after the four matches a respect grew out of it.
—JACK SHEEDY

Physicality wasn't the only thing that Dublin and Meath had to offer. Their recent history showed that they were two of the most glamorous teams in Irish sport. They were the two Leinster teams most likely to dominate the game in the province by sheer weight of playing numbers. If all the teams registered by their affiliates were to field, Meath could mobilise 1,700 adult footballers and 2,670 youths. Dublin could tog out 2,800 adults and 6,000 graded players. Kildare, the only county threatening their dominance, had only 800 adult footballers and 2,100 graded players. In 1991 Meath had 126 registered clubs, 108 adult football teams and 178 youth teams. Dublin had 234 clubs, 186 adult and 400 youth teams. Only Cork, with 267 adult and 605 youth teams, had more.

Kerry, Mayo and Tyrone had the same number of adult football teams as Meath.

The playing numbers in Dublin masked the inability of Gaelic football to penetrate the city.

———

We don't want half the county to be a suburb of Dublin.
—FRANK O'BRIEN, Meath county manager, 19 June 1991

Co. Meath in 1991 was seeking a new identity. Seán Boylan helped give it one.

The county had a population of 105,370, two-thirds the level of 2006, and it was engaging in a serious fight for its identity as well as for its livelihood. The traditional agri-food industry—of which Kepak was one of the more visible components—that had fuelled the local economy was in decline, although it still formed a large part of the county GAA psyche. 'The cows won't wait for milking for any football match,' the GAA public relations officer, Brendan Cummins, replied when there were suggestions that the starting time for the second match should be moved to 5:30 p.m. for live television purposes.

Various industries, including Navan Carpets, NEC Microchips and Dromone Engineering in Oldcastle, were striving to pick up the slack. The county council was facing two thousand planning applications a year and had decided a year earlier to implement a strict 'locals only' policy, in many cases despite the opposition of its own 29-member county council.

The population of its largest towns was about to double: 11,706 in Navan, 4,411 in Ashbourne, 4,185 in Trim and 3,539 in Kells. This was well off the 2006 peaks of 24,851 (Navan), 8,528 (Ashbourne), 6,870 (Trim) and 5248 (Kells). The biggest problem was what the county manager, Frank O'Brien, called 'a frightful concentration of septic tanks.' There was often nowhere for the grey water to go. Dunshaughlin's effluent was piped an expensive twelve miles to the river.

The unemployment rate, at 17.1 per cent, was higher than the still-high national average. One of the Meath players had been laid off by a peeved employer from Co. Laois and was a celebrity recipient of unemployment assistance at Drogheda as the team embarked on their Leinster championship campaign. 'Fellows arrived in all sorts of bangers to training,' Colm O'Rourke recalled, 'the odd one having up-to-date tax and insurance, and we always looked enviously at Ulster teams when they came south for league games, virtually all driving new models.'

Few of those behind the Meath and Dublin teams saw identity as an issue in the mid 1980s. But Boylan was an exception. He played up the spiritual significance of the Hill of Tara as a training venue and made sure that players understood where the border between the two counties was. Such niceties, famously exploited in opposing ways by previous managers, such as Georgie Leahy from Co. Laois ('a ditch between Kilkenny and Laois should not make all that much difference') and Liam Griffin from Co. Wexford (who took his players off the bus on the way to the 1996 all-Ireland final to show them where the boundary was), meant little to the Dublin players. Charlie Redmond was living in Ashbourne while playing for Dublin against Meath.

———

These fellows with tractors need to be kept in their place. Lads, we're Dubs. We need to take our guns from our holsters and blow these culchies away.

—PADDY CULLEN, pre-match talk for a league match against Mayo

Dublin too was re-imagining its identity, and Paddy Cullen had helped create it. What happened in the 1974 was as much about identity as about football.

Dubliners had a nickname for themselves; the other thirty-one counties shared one. The derogatory term 'Seáinín' (also 'Seoinín'), originally applied to a little Englander because of the perception that so many English people were called John, was rendered also in English as 'Jackeen', hence 'Dublin Jackeen', later reduced simply to Jackeen. This was opposed to 'culchie', a word whose origin is unknown but is sometimes explained—perhaps fancifully—as deriving from coillte (woods) or even more fancifully from Kiltimagh, Co. Mayo, but is more likely to be a derivative of 'agricultural labourer'. The distinctions were not always clear-cut, and there were jokes about the transient nature of city heritage: what is the definition of a culchie? A Dubliner's father.

A jackeen was more of a corner boy in popular perception, promulgated by Jimmy O'Dea in the 1920s and introduced to Dáil debate by parliamentarians Daniel Morrissey in 1949 ('that cheap jibe could come from any jackeen from any street corner in Dublin') and Oliver J. Flanagan in 1944 ('I will not shut up for you, you Dublin jackeen'). It was also used in exchanges over several decades between Fintan Coogan and Noel Lemass, who Coogan repeatedly called 'jackeen'. When Lemass eventually told him after the election of the 1973 coalition Government that 'you now have the jackeen Government you were looking for', he was reflecting the widespread perception that the city folk were back in power after decades in the cold.

Could the rise of the Dublin Gaelic football team in a 'culchie' game (one of the rare references to 'culchie' in the canon of Dáil Éireann debates refers to culchies parking their cars at Croke Park) be a re-emergence of urban culture? The players seemed to think so.

Country people had been the enemy in the decades after the rise to power in 1932 of the small farmers' party, Fianna Fáil, and after the implementation of the Common Agricultural Policy after Ireland joined the EEC (now the European Union) in 1973. A drive through the decayed quays and approach roads to the city in the early 1970s announced to visitors that urban Ireland was crumbling while rural Ireland was thriving.

'Culchies' were taking Dubliners' jobs, were getting better deals in regard to grants, in education and, crucially, from the taxman: the dichotomy between the self-assessed and the PAYE systems was one of the great injustices of the 1970s. The angry youths on Hill 16 were reacting to decentralisation, IDA policies of diverting industry to the provinces and the rejection of urban culture by successive governments.

The 1973 election result was significant. The rise of the Dublin football team a year later—and the emergence of a Dublin rocker, Phil Lynott—to challenge the country and its western showbiz was the completion of a political and cultural cycle. Townies were back in control. Dubs felt that the nation had become more urbane and sophisticated.

Jimmy Keaveney recalls that

what happened to 1974 was that Shamrock Rovers were weak. Drums were gone and there was no sporting team representing Dublin . . . When we won the all-Ireland in 1974 everybody came out to support us, regardless of whether they supported GAA or not. I remember when we played a Mickey Mouse game in Wembley we were astonished at the number of Dublin fans who travelled over to London to support us.

These fans came from the new suburbs, where Myles Wright's scheme for orbital towns had transformed life in what used to be the outlying villages of the capital. The GAA was giving these new suburbs what no other sport could provide until the rise of Leinster rugby at the beginning of the twenty-first century: a common sporting team to support.

While the fans decked out in blue and filled Hill 16, the GAA club structure was straining under the pressure: Tallaght's population climbed from 1,402 in 1961 to 62,570 in 1991—it was to rise further to 92,303—and it was effectually serviced by one senior club, Thomas Davis; the population of Clondalkin, where Round Towers had plied their trade since the infancy of the association, had risen from 3,434 to 38,489 in the same thirty years; Lucan, where Sarsfields were based, had risen from 1,657 to 13,931, and it was to rise further to 37,424 in the coming fifteen years. On the north side Blanchardstown, whose St Brigid's club opened their new park in 1979, grew from 1,328 to 34,853; Swords from 1,816 to 17,705; Malahide from 2,534 to 12,088; and John O'Leary's and O'Dwyer's home town, Balbriggan, from 2,943 to 7,724. The traditional clubs strained to cope with the new population. Clubs such as Naomh Olaf, St Sylvester's, St Peregrine's, St Jude's and Ballinteer St John's were newly established or expanded beyond all recognition.

Dún Laoghaire too was burgeoning, its population having risen from 68,101 in 1961 to 180,693, with just one GAA club, Cuala Casements, catering to the needs of a community larger than the combined populations of Carlow, Leitrim, Longford and Monaghan. Half a dozen of Dublin's bigger clubs were each serving a larger population than the county boards of Leitrim or Longford.

The middle-aged men who were now mentors and selectors, and gathering for annual golf reunions, were beginning to wonder if the spirit of 1974 could ever be reproduced on the playing field. The answer is probably not, because they were looking in the wrong place.

———

If the population of 1.3 million becomes a wasteland for the GAA then you've conceded a quarter of the population of the island.

—JOHN COSTELLOE, Dublin county secretary

Much has been said of the sociology of the seventies Dubs— almost as much as about their ball skills. Most of it is overblown.

The GAA regarded Dublin as one of its stronger counties, but in reality it was one of its weakest. Per head of population, Dublin has fewer clubs that Derry, one-fifth of the penetration of Meath or Roscommon and a seventh of the penetration of Wexford.

The ability of the county team to fill Croke Park only drew attention to the inability, unusual for a European capital, of any soccer or rugby club to be able to do so. Most of those 1970s GAA spectators never considered playing the game.

The team including the economist Robbie Kelleher, the solicitor Tony Hanahoe, the doctor Pat O'Neill and the businessmen Gay O'Driscoll, Paddy Cullen, Jimmy Keaveney and Kevin Moran was not the first Dublin team to outrun 'culchies', nor were they the first to claim the game for the middle classes.

The teams of the 1950s and 60s continue to feature prominently in the front ranks of business life today. It wasn't even clear if the support had been widened beyond the level of the 1960s, when Paddy Cullen and Jimmy Keaveney began playing for the county. The gospel of GAA wasn't spread far

beyond the traditional north-side heartlands and outer
village communities. By 1991 the south suburbs were a GAA
wasteland, from Kilmacud to Cuala.

The *Irish Press* sports writer Pádraig Puirséil once told a
story of the old Dublin fan in 1974 who described these men
as 'a bunch of culchies from Marino and Terenure.'

———

> Kevin Heffernan would be so forthcoming with advice
> for everybody. And yet, if he was competing against you,
> you know his brief was to beat you. That was it. At the
> same time he would be a great man to help others trying
> to make the game better.
>
> —SEÁN BOYLAN

To listen to Kevin Heffernan and his colleagues it was almost
as if the rise of Dublin in the 1970s was accidental and had
come from the lowest of low ebbs: defeat by Louth, with
Heffernan as Dublin manager, in the 1973 championship.

In 1974, the year in which Hill 16 and a lot of other things
were invented, Dublin had one representative on the Leinster
team in February: the about-to-be-dropped George Wilson.

Jimmy Keaveney was in retirement when Dublin were
playing badly against Wexford in a curtain-raiser for Kerry
and Roscommon's league final. It was Leslie Deegan, a sub
for Fran Ryder, who changed history that year, scoring the
goal that knocked out the then big-hitters of Leinster
football, Offaly. Deegan popped up in the right place at the
right time, in the nature of other epoch-changing GAA
substitutes such as Séamus Darby and Fergal Taaffe.

Leslie's legend is one of the more unusual ones to attach
itself to the Dubs story. He goes unrecognised around the
town, while Jimmy Keaveney and Paddy Cullen are still

greeted like old friends, which they were to a generation of Dubs.

A 1970s tsunami followed: Dublin defeated Cork and Galway in 1974, Derry in 1975, Galway and Kerry in 1976 and Kerry and Armagh in 1977, shaking up the power structures in Gaelic football. Few of these games were classics, although the 1977 semi-final against Kerry attracts television audiences of more than 100,000 every time it's shown on TG4. There were more stoppages for frees in matches involving Dublin than with any other team in this era, and the free-counts for the 1975 and 1976 semi-finals are among the highest of all time. Even the 1977 semi-final was a poor match until that explosive ending, when Tony Hanahoe conjured up two late goals from David Hickey and Bernard Brogan in the last six minutes. (Hanahoe later achieved something even more spectacular: he was responsible for the rule changes that make today's football much more exciting.)

There is a consensus among opponents and supporters alike about why Dublin came to dominate in the mid-1970s. As Gay O'Driscoll, who had been around since 1966, pointed out, 'four or five players made all the difference to the team.' Dublin introduced a professional level of training at a time when standards were ludicrously low. It took a while for others to catch up, but catch up they did. By 1991 many intermediate club teams were training as often as the county teams of those days.

Afterwards there were further audacious escapes, against Offaly in 1979 and Wicklow in 1981, that have been conveniently forgotten by all but those from Offaly and Wicklow. But huge victories over inadequately prepared opposition gave the supporters a chance to celebrate their superiority.

In 1983 Heffo was back, Mullins was back, Tommy Drumm was back—but the Dubs didn't look all-Ireland material. In 1963 the team of 1958 was about to break up. Des Ferguson was persuaded out of retirement.

The pattern here says a lot about Dublin's football team. A stunt, a stroke and a player called out of retirement lifts the confidence of the rest of the lads, and once the Dubs get some momentum going they take a lot of stopping.

In 1991 they stopped themselves.

Did these guys really believe that Cosgrove's free would go over? that Redmond's penalties would go in? that Meath wouldn't come snatching back at another lost match and defeat them in the end?

Defeat and victory could be treated almost the same, because the issue was identity.

On the temple that Hill 16 became at that time, something much deeper than football was being worshipped.

———

> It can be said that it was a disappointing game in the football sense but for the singing, chanting, banner-waving supporters at the Stretford (sorry Hill 16) and Canal ends that was of little consequence.
>
> —BOB HYLAND, *Irish Independent*, 23 September 1974

There was another reason why the Dublin team of the 1970s was so feted in the city. As the only part of the country with access to BBC television, while the rest languished in one-channel land, Dublin was acutely aware that it had no sporting equivalent of the English and Scottish soccer clubs, no outlets for expression of urban sporting identity.

Dubliners were beginning to use the new ferry services, introduced after 1966, for travelling to the Spion Kop and Stretford End to support English soccer clubs. They wanted a Stretford End of their own; they wanted to sing and chant and throw things on the field like their cousins in Manchester and Liverpool.

League of Ireland soccer partly served the purpose for their fathers until the 1950s, but partition and penury had killed its potential. The supporters flocked to Dalymount Park for chaotic and dangerous showpiece events: the 1946 match against England, 1947 against Spain, 1953 against France, 1962 against Austria and an otherwise forgotten 1970s Shamrock Rovers versus Manchester United exhibition, with George Best just back from his Miss World affray, in which the crowd spilled onto the pitch, and the rusting roof of the shed threatened to collapse under the strain of supporters.

Rugby was highly successful at the national level, but it was too exclusive and school-based at the club level. Crowds didn't chant at rugby matches, and when they sang it tended towards parlour music: Alive, alive-o.

The GAA, built on identity, provided a place to turn to for the urban children of Lemass's Ireland, and when Dublin beat Wexford in the 1974 championship those city kids aligned their identity with the GAA almost by accident.

Hill 16 became the Stretford End by the time Dublin played Cork in the 1974 all-Ireland semi-final. Songs were borrowed from the English terraces ('Come on, you boys in blue', 'Nice one, Jimmy, nice one, son'), and Dublin's cabaret culture added a vibrant musical tradition of its own.

Until the Dubs did it, county scarves were not worn at GAA matches, supporters didn't sing communal songs and flags were handkerchief size. The Dubs brought the GAA from the days of crepe hats to a 1970s cult as great as Thin Lizzy and greatcoats.

It wasn't unusual for cabaret artists to have new songs ready for each victory. Songs such as 'The Jacks Are Back', 'The Likes of Heffo's Army' (by the Memories) and 'Heffo's Heroes' (sung by the Light Blues: 'Here go Heffo's heroes to play a good game') crept in amid the glam rockers to the Irish charts.

The fans who came in 1974 stayed even when the supply of all-Irelands came to a halt in 1977, leaving them with only two all-Ireland victories since. All the 1991 Dublin selectors were seventies men: from the pantheon and above challenge or question by the new generation.

When Paddy Cullen was appointed Dublin manager in 1990 the fans imagined that Heffo's heroes might be returning, by proxy, to play a good game. Let the good times roll, indeed.

Chapter 4 ∾

RULES OF ENGAGEMENT

Our game is naturally violent. It is an unabashed, no-holds-barred physical contest. Violence, in both thought and deed, has always been an essential part of our great game—which, we should quickly enforce, is also honourable and manly in impressive measures.

——LIAM HAYES, January 1997

By June 1991 the Dublin and Meath footballers had worked out the perfect ways of winding each other up. Dublin-Meath matches in the 1980s were among the least attractive and best attended. The reason was clear to all but admitted by few: the prospect of a row between two committed, aggressive teams prepared to disregard the rules at the first opportunity.

How this came about is a topic that has evaded any serious analysis and has instead become the subject of conjecture and anecdote.

———

Dancing is a contact sport. Football is a hitting sport.
——A Meath footballer quoted by the journalist David Walsh
before Dublin v. Meath, 2 June 1991

So who was to blame? Who had started the tradition of softening up an opponent, of intimidation, of pulling, dragging and off-the-ball antagonism?

If, as is often claimed, familiarity breeds contempt, the Dublin-Meath saga began from a bad place.

Meath had won two championships and two leagues in four years. They had won four Leinster titles. Dublin had a reputation to uphold: a reputation for looking after themselves. Dubliners of a certain age will tell you that they had to toughen up to protect themselves from the country lads.

In the early days, club and county GAA was dominated by vocational clubs, made up of country employees in various professions, including the drapery trade, breweries and the Gardaí. In the second period of the association's history Dublin football drew its strength from the rural clubs, mainly in the north of the county. In the third it drew from indigenous urban residents and the population of the new suburbs.

The 1942 Dublin team was largely made up of rural players from the outlying villages. This was never true of another Dublin team.

Each stage was progressively less successful for honours won—two-thirds of Dublin's all-Irelands were won before 1926—but it did lead to a greater level of participation and a greater connection and more traditional ties with the community. The steeling of Dublin has sometimes been dated to the third stage, the arrival of the St Vincent's team on the scene in 1949.

After 1949 St Vincent's dominated football from their Marino stronghold, the GAA invading every aspect of the culture in the parish in a way that urban clubs had seldom ever done in Dublin but had done in Cork and Belfast.

Most famously, in 1953 fourteen St Vincent's players and the Air Corps goalkeeper, Peadar O'Grady, outplayed Cavan, the all-Ireland champions, to win the national league.

St Vincent's are credited with providing five all-Ireland

inter-county titles for Dublin, those of 1958, 1963, 1974, 1976 and 1977, as well as two all-Ireland club titles, four Leinster titles and twenty-five Dublin titles. The club supplied four managers to Dublin. Along the way, and at an early stage, some of their stronger personalities earned a new reputation for hardness to the county team.

Some people say the aggression dates to one club match against St Mary's, when the Vincent's players, on cue, all punched their opposite number as they paraded out of the dressing-room.

Some say the aggression was honed in mud-spattered battles against Offaly in the early 1960s, including the famous episode of a stone thrown into the crowd by a Dublin player in Portlaoise in 1961, a match in which 'immediately the pitch was the scene of a hundred battles,' according to the sports writer John D. Hickey.

As we shall see, there was method in their malevolence, this metropolitan malevolence from Marino.

You do what you have to, I'll look after them in Steevens' on Monday
—Dublin 1970s footballer and 1991 selector PAT O'NEILL

By the time Kevin Heffernan took over as Dublin manager, toughness was a tactic. Dublin had a general policy in the team that if any man was being bullied, another Dublin player, not his marker, would sort him out. Retribution should never be a task for an immediate opponent, who would be in a position to retaliate as soon as the referee was distracted. It was delegated to a colleague, and often that colleague was Brian Mullins.

When David Walsh compiled a seminal memoir of the

Dublin team of the 1970s for the 1988 incarnation of the magazine *Magill*, John McCarthy told Walsh a story about the league semi-final between Dublin and Tyrone at Croke Park in May 1975.

It was a tough, physical game, won easily by Dublin—they beat Meath in the final—with David Hickey, in particular, singled out for hard marking. McCarthy was marked by a small corner back who, he says, punched him during the playing of the national anthem, saying, 'I'm Mickey Joe Forbes, the hardest wee mon in Ulster, hit me, hit me.' McCarthy looked at the smaller Forbes and suspected that if he touched him he was going to get sent off. As the game progressed he kept hitting him, all the time repeating, 'I'm Mickey Joe Forbes, the hardest wee mon in Ulster, hit me, hit me.'

According to McCarthy, he ran towards the Dublin dugout and asked what he should do but was told to keep running, not to get involved. Brian Mullins got the ball and swept Mickey Joe Forbes aside as he embarked on a solo run. 'As he was being taken off,' McCarthy said, 'I wanted to run over and say, "Now, Mickey Joe Forbes, the hardest wee mon in Ulster, you have just met the hardest wee mon in Leinster."'

Good story. But Forbes wasn't substituted in the match. It was part of the mythology that grew around the Dubs of the time, and Kevin Heffernan's philosophy was that in an era of man-marking most serious retribution had to be done by another man's marker.

The 1991 Dublin team was run by 1970s players. When Keith Barr fouled Colm O'Rourke in the third match in 1991 he made an escape over to the end line and had to be pursued by the referee, Tommy Howard, like a Wild West sheriff, who stopped to identify six separate players, turning players around and noting their jersey numbers until he found the fugitive Barr.

We're talking about battlefields. Violence and honour hand in hand. It's a game not easily enjoyed on the field. It's a game which regularly strikes apprehension, and often fear, into the hearts of participants and observers.

—LIAM HAYES, January 1997

Anybody who grew up in Co. Meath in the 1970s quickly learnt that Dublin is the centre of the country, not Tara. They also learnt that any footballer on the Dublin team is automatically three inches taller.

Part of the problem was the sports writers. Dublin has more of them, and when a Dublin team does moderately well they write eulogies that make the team seem better than it is.

To sit in the press box for the replayed match between Dublin and Meath in 1983 was to be part of an exercise in partisanship. Downey, Carroll, O'Brien silent in their assessment; Pat Roche of the *Irish Times* and Bob Hyland of the *Irish Independent* giving running commentaries on the game, the blindness of the referee to Meath's indiscretions, the brilliance of the Dubs.

Even when Dublin were among the worst teams in Leinster, the Dublin writers transformed them into some sort of national treasure by means of hilarious stories of their ineptitude. When other counties go through bad patches it's regarded as an embarrassment; when Dublin go through one their failures are transformed into a soap opera for the evening newspaper.

Four decades is long enough to create a pretty substantial foundation legend for the Dubs: the disorganisation of the pre-Heffo days, the Kevin Heffernan team talk that day they lost against Louth in the 1973 Leinster championship.

In response, Meath had a foundation myth of their own

that dated from before Boylan's arrival in 1982. The team of the 1960s was expected to go far, and they did—to Australia, in fact. In the decade when the cult of celebrity was visiting the GAA ground as well as the dancehalls and spanking new television studios in Montrose, the distinctively red-headed Pat 'Red' Collier had created a rapport with the fans. There's one in each decade in each sport, and Red was the man of the 1960s. A Simon Geoghegan, Damien Duff or Jayo of his generation, he liked to sally out of defence and, even though he was less than five feet six, knock bigger men out of his way, famously planting the Cork midfielder Mick Burke in the 1967 all-Ireland final in an incident that many suspect turned the match in Meath's favour.

Meath had snatched a league title from under the noses of Heffo's Heroes in 1976. But they had their fair share of trauma after that: three Leinster final defeats, and all the confidence of the county seemed to have drained with the Boyne water by the time they lost to Wexford and Longford in consecutive championship matches.

Key players of the Leinster finals of the 1970s, Gerry McEntee and Colm O'Rourke among them, were getting older and more frustrated with each passing year. O'Rourke told his team-mates that Dublin would have no illusions that they could beat Meath. They were expected to put up a good show, and that was that.

They weren't good enough. And, more importantly, they weren't tough enough.

————

The spirit which new coach Seán Boylan has instilled in the squad was very noticeable in a hectic second half and if only he can get them to play with such fire and vigour for the full hour the future of the county team might be

more rosy than most people seem to think.
—PAUL CLARKE, report on Meath v. Galway,
Meath Chronicle, November 1982

Longevity in the game has served Seán Boylan well. He has become revered as the archetypal GAA team manager. There is a statue erected in his honour outside a hotel in his native Dunboyne. His managerial skills are spoken about with reverence. Only twice in his innings, among the longest in modern GAA history, was he challenged for the job of team manager. The dignity and approachability he showed towards the fans, the media and those who had just a passing interest seem, even at a short remove, to be from another age.

The story of how the hurling coach and football team masseur was appointed manager in September 1982, 'because no one else wanted the job', has been mythologised beyond recognition. Eugene McGee recalls the first time he heard about 'this hurling fellow who had recently taken over the Meath football team, because nobody else wanted the job and somebody had to do it.'

Like many GAA legends, it's half true. Nobody wanted the job, because it didn't exist. The job Boylan took in 1982 was like that of Fran Ryder, not that of Paddy Cullen.

According to Boylan,

I never called myself the manager . . . The term was relatively new at the time. I was essentially the coach/trainer, answerable to the county board and six selectors, a cumbersome arrangement which would ultimately cause problems. I would have observed from afar Kevin Heffernan, Mick O'Dwyer and Eugene McGee. They had a huge influence, not just in the counties that they looked after but all around the country. It was a different role.

This was the old approach. GAA trainers put the cones on the field and organised the laps. GAA managers booked the hotel and made sure everyone got to the game on time. The GAA coach was the vehicle that brought the team to the game. It was also part of the reason for Meath having just lost to Wexford and Longford in consecutive championships.

Boylan doesn't give himself enough credit. There was debate and suspicion within the GAA about the very soccer-sounding role of 'manager'. (Jack Mahon in his column in *Gaelic Sport* used to complain that it was 'borrowed'.) Galway went into the 1983 all-Ireland final without a recognised manager. Tyrone had two before the 1986 all-Ireland. By the mid 1980s it was unthinkable that a successful county team could operate without a manager rather than a coach-trainer. More than Heffernan, O'Dwyer and McGee, Boylan is the one who achieved this. He was supported in doing so by the most charismatic of the current players, Colm O'Rourke, a close friend of McGee and a supporter of the new managerial system. The oft-told story of how O'Rourke used to say, 'We will make a manager of Boylan yet' had more truth than either man was prepared to admit. One of Boylan's opponents for the coaching job later regretted his withdrawal as the role grew in stature.

Being a selector was a different matter. There were fifteen candidates for the selection committee just for the job of coach-trainer, which seemed a lot more hassle than it was worth. Boylan got the job when Mattie Kerrigan, Gerry McEntee and his predecessor, Mick O'Brien, withdrew.

Boylan says he talked over his role with Brian Smith until 2 a.m. the night before the convention and agreed to take the job for a few months until they found someone else.

It would be only fair to say that I took it on a stopgap until they got someone better to do it. I had huge limitations and still have, but I would be a good listener and always have done, people who had gone through it themselves, who had played at the top, people who looked after teams that had played at the top. They hadn't won a Leinster since 1970. They hadn't won an all-Ireland since 1967. They had won a great national league in 1975, but beaten in a Leinster final in 1976 and 1977, so it went down low again.

Boylan had a political advantage over any other candidate. He was already popular with the delegates and had proved able to look after himself on the hurling field and, more importantly, in the cut and thrust of county board politics. He knew how Meath clubs voted; he knew how their minds worked.

His political astuteness eventually enabled him to become the game's longest-serving manager with a single county.

Colm O'Rourke, already a power-broker in the county, spoke at the meeting at which he was appointed, expressing support and calling for the co-operation of the county board with the team management on matters such as mid-week club matches.

———

The people we were playing against, they didn't eat any more potatoes than we did.
—SEÁN BOYLAN recalls what he said at his first team talk

At the end of September 1982 Boylan walked into his first Meath dressing-room. He gave a pretty standard introductory address, familiar to GAA county managers everywhere, about how, when they came in to a dressing-room, they all came in as Meathmen, and how it didn't matter where they came from within the county, whether it was from Oldcastle or Dunboyne or Laytown, even though they would have been very competitive against each other on a Sunday. He established the collaborative mentality that every sports manager needs but that was absent from the Meath teams he had watched lose Leinster finals in the 1970s.

Then he revealed his secret, the devastatingly simple core belief that was to serve Seán Boylan for nearly two decades as a football coach and motivator—a St John's Wort of football management so simple that it defied contradiction:

> If you can play well for five minutes, then, with practice, you can play well for eight minutes, and gradually progress. It is a question of getting the body physically ready and then developing the mentality to be able to concentrate for a particular length of time.

He won some of them over immediately. Others took a little longer to crack. Eventually they all came round.

> My job was to get them fit to play at top level, realise you can't store fitness, realise it's something that has to be worked at and, if they do get injured, to realise the effect that it will have on their muscles.

He was dealing with players who were far more experienced than he was, who had competed against very good Dublin teams and had never got the major honours.

> I took that whole group with me, so it was a big thing that we won Leinster in 1986. It was a major thing. They would have done anything for the county . . . You have to use the two, brains and muscles. Asking a man to do something he is not able to do, to give him instruction and he fails,

it is not his fault. We are all guilty of asking him to do something and he is not the person to do that job. But sometimes it is only trial and error. He will get a shot at it and will relish some responsibility. Others don't want to know. They are still great footballers. But they mightn't make it the whole way.

I played on a Meath hurling team that lost to Kilkenny by 33 points, but I was out in the front field the next day pucking a ball and out with the club the night after, because it was about the love of the game.

—SEÁN BOYLAN

Outside Meath, Boylan was unknown. Hurling was his sport, as it was for many in Dunboyne in his childhood. His father, a 1916 man, a War of Independence veteran and a Fine Gael activist, had helped revive the club and steer it through its most successful period, eighty years earlier.

Young Seán was on the county hurling teams from when he was a minor and had been a nominee for various county board positions from the mid 1970s, on the disciplinary committee and with officerships in the fractious hurling board, where he became deputy chair.

Boylan wasn't a manager in the sense that Mick O'Dwyer, Kevin Heffernan or Eugene McGee had been, but he knew how to turn a coaching job into a management one.

The fact that the masseur was now coach was the cause of raised eyebrows outside Co. Meath, but in October 1978 Boylan had been appointed coach-trainer of the hurling team, succeeding Dessie Ferguson. He continued playing, coming on in midfield and trying, unsuccessfully, to disrupt the midfield dominance of Tom Johnson against Kildare in

1979, and he was being selected by the junior hurlers as late as 1984. He learnt a lot from his hurling days.

> If you are defeated it doesn't mean we are failures. That is something that I have learnt to take, if you were involved as long as I was with hurling in Meath. We would have known a lot of defeat and big defeats. You'd get up and have a go again at it the next day.

He learnt how the coach-trainer role could evolve. But he lost faith. In he came, back from a World Health Organisation conference in 1982.

> It cost me an extra £130 to change the ticket, to make it back for training. And there were only seven people there. That finished me with Meath hurling.

Funnily enough, he had three people more at his training session than Mick O'Brien had from the footballers before their 1982 championship defeat against Longford. Boylan was to change that.

———

> Sometimes I'll look at the lads and I'll know what I planned for them is all wrong. I'll just tear it up in my head and start again.
>
> —SEÁN BOYLAN

For seven years Boylan built up Meath's stamina with the sort of rigorous endurance training that the players had only read about.

They ran in the freezing water at Bettystown strand in March, surged up the sand-dunes and followed a sapping course up the Hill of Tara by the light of torches. In 1990 he had them rowing on the Grand Canal between Summerhill and Kilcock and then running a five-furlong horse-training gallop covered in wood shavings, with the final furlong uphill, Cheltenham-style. In 1991, when Boylan worked out that the accumulated injuries of five years on the road together made endurance training impossible, he put them into the Gormanston College swimming-pool with buoyancy aids. Boylan built up trust with the players, made them believe in him and themselves. He remained loyal to them, even when games became nasty and they got involved. The players regarded him as obsessive. After two Leinster final defeats in 1997 and 1998 he had them training for eleven day-and-night sessions in succession before the first round of the 1999 championship against Wicklow. How badly did they want to win? They went on to win the all-Ireland that year.

For one whole session he had them falling on the ground and bouncing back up again, having decided that they had a tendency to lie down too long after going to ground. For Boylan,

> speed and fitness go together . . . If you overdo one without looking for the other, you pay the price. I have been involved in eight all-Ireland finals, including two replays. But I would never have done a sprint with any team for at least ten weeks before an all-Ireland final. Now I never have closed training sessions, so people can see it for themselves, but I don't want to tell the country . . . People have all sorts of stories about Meath football and what they do and what they don't do. But I never have a closed training session. People can see for themselves what we do. We are able to survive on crumbs because we are so familiar with it . . . People used to say I had an entourage with me, but it was important to have a

masseur, a doctor. It was important the food was right. There was no point in training if you're not going to eat the right food.

He did have an entourage of selectors, a county secretary and chairman and four fellow selectors. It made decision-making cumbersome during matches—the equivalent of a county board decision on the sideline. A sub, Neil O'Sullivan, was warmed up three times during the 1984 Leinster final while the selection committee tried to agree about bringing him on or not. In 1985 Boylan obtained agreement from the county board to pick his own selectors.

————

All I wanted to do was to help players to achieve excellence and see them do it. I was fortunate enough to be around teams that were in seven all-Ireland finals and won four— fortunate to be able to help them get there.

—SEÁN BOYLAN

Any progress Meath made would be measured against Dublin: were they able to match their football? and were they able to match their toughness?

At first glance, the pre-Deadlock story of Meath seems like that of a messianic manager, steady progress—first round near-miss, provincial final, all-Ireland semi-final—and ultimate success.

Meath people felt they didn't deserve to lose to Dublin in the replayed provincial quarter-finals of 1983. They came out of it with a reputation for naïvety and softness. According to Boylan,

they needed to get tough . . . They had no divine right to

it . . . Talk about the tradition in our county that was there, and there was a great tradition; over 35 years the county had quite an amount of success. But it was up to those lads that they had to do it for themselves. They had to make their tradition. It wasn't a question of proving it to the great players that had gone before. They had to prove it to themselves. We set about to create as best we could the environment for that to happen.

A glance at successive team pictures shows the growing thighs and biceps that turned Meath into the superheroes of the 1990s, waiting to sap the energy out of anyone who would try to outplay them and coming back to beat them in the second period of injury time. According to Colm O'Rourke, he wasn't strong enough to take the hits in the early days.

O'Rourke remembers how in 1983 Meath were leading Dublin with a minute to go as he gained possession on the Hogan Stand side and was heading unopposed towards the canal goal with a score at his mercy. At the last second he hesitated between going for a goal and a point. By the time he decided to tap it over the bar Mick Kennedy appeared, blocked his kick, and the ball was transferred quickly downfield, where Dublin got a free on the railway goal. Barney Rock pointed and the game finished on the kick-out.

A goalkeeping mistake and an own goal had given Dublin a draw they hardly deserved, 2-8 each. Five minutes into the replay the new goalkeeper smothered the ball but allowed it to escape and trickle over his line for a goal—Dublin won by 3-9 to 0-16 in extra time, with an Anton O'Toole goal after another mistake. Like the rest of the country, the defeated Meath camp marvelled at how Dublin snatched an all-Ireland from Galway.

Marvelled is hardly the word. The country was horrified, as Dublin won with twelve men, having had three players sent off and having instigated a tunnel brawl to sort out Galway's midfielder, Brian Talty. Galway lost focus and allowed the match to slip away in the second half. The message to all of Dublin's opponents was clear: disregard for the rules of the game is no barrier to success.

———

I think the games we had with Meath in the late 1980s did nothing for the GAA. There was a lot of off-the-ball stuff going on, something that we cannot really be proud of, but when we look back now we can say we left a great legacy in these four games.

—CHARLIE REDMOND

Meath won a trophy in 1984, the Centenary Cup, important at the time but soon to be forgotten; but Mick Lyons's broken thumb meant that Meath didn't get out of the starting-blocks in a Leinster final played on the hottest day of the year.

Lyons finished that year with a new reputation for toughness, largely acquired in the compromise-rules series against Australia in October. He was flattened in Cork, but he showed that he could look after himself in the second match in Croke Park. The legend of Lyons, Lyons the tamer (the square was known as Lyons' Den), was born that day. His sending off in the second leg of Deadlock was only the second of his career; he had fallen victim to a short-lived crackdown on personal fouls in a league match in 1984.

Meath didn't get to play Dublin in 1985, having slipped to two Laois goals in the Leinster semi-final, losing by 2-11 (Meath 0-7) in Tullamore on a day on which Liam Harnan and Brian Stafford were both injured. Paschal Doran scored the first goal for Laois, and when John Costelloe returned the kick-out with the defence hopelessly out of place Willie

Brennan scored the second. The defeat nearly cost Boylan his job. He was opposed by Paul Kenny for the managership—no more talk of coach-trainer—but a timely intervention by Colm O'Rourke and Joe Cassells saved the day.

In 1986 Meath began their period of domination of Dublin by 0-9 to 0-7, as Barney Rock was taken off injured and Joe Cassells tamed Dublin's wandering Tommy Carr. Newcomer David Beggy told an incredulous Mick Dunne that he had been in Croke Park just once before, for a U2 concert. Their run came to an end with a three-player mix-up in the Meath goalmouth that allowed Ger Power to grab what was later seen as the vital goal, the turning point of the game. It was high farce. Brian Stafford was dispossessed out the field. Ogie Moran drilled a hopeful ball forward. Mick Lyons, Joe Cassells and Mickey McQuillan all decided to go for the one ball. Roguishly, Lyons tried to push Ger Power (of Kerry) out of the way but collided instead with the advancing McQuillan, while Cassells was tripped by Lyons's outstretched leg. The ball bounced helpfully into Power's path.

Meath won two more encounters with Dublin, by 1-13 to 0-12 in 1987 (Mattie McCabe scored the first goal, and Meath came from behind) and 2-5 to 0-9 in 1988 (when Charlie Redmond missed a last-minute penalty for Dublin). Dublin won 2-12 to 1-10 with Vinnie Murphy's late goal in 1989, and Meath won 1-14 to 0-14 in 1990, when a rare and controversial goal by Meath's Colm O'Rourke brought it to an end. Colm Brady's high kick for a point was held or brought back by the wind, and, as it lazily dropped close to the crossbar, Colm O'Rourke arrived to worry John O'Leary and force a goal. The officials ruled that it was a goal, and a goal it stayed.

The level of interest was high by the standards of the time. The 56,051 that showed up at the Leinster final in 1984 was a 22-year record for the province, the second-highest championship attendance of that summer and twice the attendance at the 1981 Leinster final. The attendances of 43,763 in 1986, 48,122 in 1987, 42,302 in 1988, 56,839 in 1989 and 53,847 in 1990 were each among the three highest of the year, with those in 1988 and 1990 bettered only by the attendance at the all-Ireland final.

Rivalries were always good for GAA ticket sales, as they were when Meath jousted with Louth and Cavan in the 1940s and 50s or when Dublin jousted with Kerry in the 1970s, and with Offaly and Kildare in Leinster. But this rivalry was to become more famous than any of them.

————

Let the good times roll again.
—PADDY CULLEN, newly appointed Dublin manager, October
1990

While Boylan was now a veteran of Dublin-Meath encounters, Dublin's new manager, Paddy Cullen, was a relative newcomer. He was no stranger to the big occasion, but only as a player. He was the original Dublin poster boy, the first Dublin player to feature in the magazine *Solo* in 1973, long before he had saved the Liam Sammon penalty that inspired his colleagues to the first of three all-Ireland titles in 1974.

He made his Dublin debut at full-forward against Derry in a challenge game on the eve of the Galway-Meath 1966 all-Ireland final, and he marked the occasion by breaking his ankle after only five minutes. When he returned, on the urging of his lifelong friend Jimmy Keaveney, it was as a goalkeeper, having turned down the chance to play League of Ireland soccer with Shelbourne.

He began serving his time as an electrician with

McNaughton's at the age of fifteen in 1960, joined Merchants' Warehousing and spent his working day fixing cranes that hung over the River Liffey. He worked for a Swiss company, Brown Boveri, in Dundrum from 1969 to 1978 and left only when Lister's came along with an offer he couldn't refuse. They wanted him to supervise the sales of electrical generators, and the salary was too good to pass up.

Within a year Cullen left Lister's to become personnel officer at Musgrave's Cash and Carry 'soon after the 1978 final, which was not ideal.' His place in history was defined by that Mikey Sheehy goal in 1978. 'I tell him that I made him a star; he will say that he made me a millionaire.' It was a builder friend, Tony O'Donnell, who persuaded him to cash in on the notoriety from that incident and to purchase a pub in Ballsbridge, which still bears his name, although he sold it in 1994 (along with his name) to run the Manor Inn in Swords.

Cullen has had a lot of time to think about the incident that defined his career.

There is no doubt in my mind the free for the goal originated from an earlier incident between myself and Ger Power. On the first occasion, I cleared the ball, and I felt Ger had come in late on me. As he was walking away I clipped his ankle. The referee didn't see it, but a lot of people in the crowd did, and they started booing me. The next time the ball came, I collected it and passed it off, and the two of us just bumped into one another. Then I heard the whistle blow, and I honestly thought it was a free out for us; I mean, I had been in possession of the ball . . . I couldn't believe it when the free went to them. I was saying, 'Hold on a minute, here,' but, before I knew it, Mikey Sheehy was placing the ball and chipping it into the net . . . What disappointed me is that everyone involved in that famous incident has gone into the pros and cons, but Séamus Aldridge has not answered the basic criticisms levelled at him . . . It was I who was fouled. It should have been a free out to Dublin instead of a free in. And, most importantly of all, as the foul allegedly took place inside the fourteen yards line, the ball should have been placed by the referee and not by a player, as when taking a quick free outfield.

Cullen retired as Dublin goalkeeper suddenly after winning a fourth All Star award in 1979 to began a high-profile innings as Dublin's favourite GAA publican, with Sheehy's boots and a framed sequence of the Sheehy goal on display in the bar. Twelve years later came the phone call that placed him once more at the heart of Dublin football and dragged him into the story of the 1991 Deadlock.

Coup Cullen.
—*Evening Herald* headline when Paddy Cullen was appointed
manager of Dublin

The phone call was a total surprise, for Cullen himself as well as for the perennial Dublin manager-speculation industry. In August 1990 he was appointed Dublin manager for the GAA equivalent of a one-year contract. The shortness of the contract reflected the mistrust of the county board and their difficulty in deciding who should get the job.

Cullen wasn't the first choice—that was Tony Hanahoe— or even the fifth choice. Two months elapsed, and the start of the national football league was approaching before they found a manager.

Hanahoe was followed by Kevin Heffernan, Bobby Doyle,

Brian Mullins, Alan Larkin, Pat O'Neill and Jim Brogan. When Hanahoe said no, Kevin Heffernan pondered over proposals that the national league would be rescheduled for spring—then said no. Gay O'Driscoll said he wasn't interested. Bobby Doyle also refused. Mickey Whelan, Alan Larkin, Pat O'Neill and Jim Brogan were still in the race.

Word came that the county board would make an announcement on Monday evening, 24 September 1990. The two who were to become Cullen's selectors, Pat O'Neill and Jim Brogan, were led to believe that Mullins would be manager.

After the *Evening Herald* headline on the day, 'Brian's Job?' suggested that Mullins was poised to take over as Dublin's new senior football manager, the Dublin County Board decided to postpone a decision—some say as a result of the newspaper leak. It was only then that Jim King contacted Cullen at the Listowel Races and offered him the job. He said he'd have to think about it. Twenty-four hours later Paddy Cullen said yes. The decision was announced on the following Monday, 1 October 1990.

Later it was stated that Mullins had taken over as director of juvenile affairs in his club, and the timing didn't suit. Others claimed that Cullen won because of his diplomacy. He was popular with fans and was presentable. The sponsors—or, indeed, would-be sponsors, for Kaliber never got the gig—liked him.

Cullen accepted the job offer without expressing too much optimism. 'I want to try and get a bunch of fellows and harness them into a unit that will eventually meet the required challenge. In other words I want a bit of success, and I believe we have the nucleus to do that.' Fran Ryder was offered the position of trainer and accepted. Pat O'Neill and Jim Brogan became his fellow selectors. 'I'm just the mouthpiece,' Paddy said, always good for the sound-bite;

'they have the brains.' A 'GAA Jack Charlton,' Tom O'Riordan called him, 'prepared to speak his own mind.'

———

When Paddy drove into his first training session in a yellow Merc, toting a fat cigar, he brought a touch of Ron Atkinson to drab Parnell Park.

—TOM O'RIORDAN, 7 October 1990

The newspapers pointed out that no previous Dublin manager had ever had to face a first-round tie against the reigning provincial champions.

The blazers of Belvedere Square didn't realise it, but the fans were already excited. Paddy Cullen, with no managerial experience, was still the poster boy ten years after he had retired and twenty-five years after he had first played for Dublin. He was charismatic in a way that his predecessors Heffo, Hanahoe, Mullins and McCaul never were—the wisecracking conquistador of Kerrymen of old getting ready for a new battle.

People *liked* him. People even loved him. He was a PR dream—a star of the 'Lifestyle' pages as well as the sports pages.

That was in October. In November, Cullen told Joe McNally to lose two stone or he was off the team. McNally was dropped, along with two other all-Ireland medallists, Ciarán Duff and Barney Rock, leaving the 1983 gallant crew, as in the 'Irish Rover', reduced down to two: John O'Leary and Gerry Hargan.

Cullen told the team that he wanted a more direct game: players who would fight for the ball, chase and chase and not take easy options and run into space when the opposition had the ball. 'We need ball-winners; I want players thinking and playing with the same fire as teams from the past.'

Of the eighty players he selected for a series of trial matches in Parnell Park, only one failed to show up.

Chapter 5

PLAYERS AND WATCHERS

All the players involved, the 64 or 65 players, their names need to be etched in stone because of what they did for Gaelic football. They brought it to a new league.

—SEÁN BOYLAN

The GAA has always been jumpy about the number of players that should be allowed on a county panel. Big panels cost more and cause problems for legislators. The county panel is now capped at 26. Deadlock shows that that might not be not big enough for an amateur game. Meath used 31 players, Dublin had 26. In 1996 Meath won an all-Ireland using 19 players. Kerry had won the 1978 all-Ireland championship by playing three matches. Meath needed four to win the first round and ten to reach the 1991 final.

The dedication required of an inter-county footballer was enormous in an era when collective training still took precedence over gym work and personal training, and when fitness had been increased to a professional level in an amateur game. Working in their jobs by day, these footballers led an interior life, a parallel spiritual life of sacrifices and sacred groves. Football took over every waking hour as it did their leisure time throughout the year.

Seán Boylan tells the story of how he once gave his panel an unexpected Sunday off. The players' wives were on the phone telling him never to do that again: the guys were unbearable. Being home on Sunday ruined the family routine.

Sometimes employers were co-operative, sometimes not. Tommy Carr was on a very strict army course at the time. He was called to the office and was told that whatever time off he wanted he could have, because the game was coming up. On the other side, a few years earlier one Meath player lost his job because of his football commitments.

The players shattered all the stereotypes associated with Gaelic games. They even crossed borders. Liam Hayes lived in Lucan, where Jack Sheedy lived, though the two had never met. Charlie Redmond was in Meath, greeting neighbours, shopkeepers and commuters while he broke their hearts on Sunday afternoons with his free-taking. Great sporting rivalries were not supposed to be like this.

———

Meath appear to show signs of wear and tear. They appear to have lost that fraction of a yard and even the appetite for winning. I'm beginning to wonder have we seen the end of this Meath team.

—TONY HANAHOE, December 1990

In Meath the fans liked the mix. They depicted their farmers and builders as the tough men and the soft town boys as the ones who were fast on their feet. But the reality was that this team were on the road for a long time. Despite them having won for the previous five years it was, for Liam Hayes,

beginning to peter out. Some lads were going to retire, I

was going to retire in my own mind, Mick Lyons was going to retire, Gerry Mac was going to retire, other lads like Rourkie and Bernard Flynn and Bernie were going to go on, but they were on their last legs.

Mick McQuillan shared a home town with Dublin's John O'Leary, and it was rumoured that the two exchanged dark secrets when nobody was looking. McQuillan also escaped from the posts to play midfield for his club when nobody was looking. (Meath goalkeepers had a bad name after 1983.)

Robbie O'Malley had spent most of his summers learning how to play the guitar, and he could be spotted at Rossnaree Hotel ballad sessions on Friday nights.

Mick Lyons spent the early part of his career trying to find a way of frightening off forwards without anyone holding it against him. He succeeded eventually in the 1984 compromise rules, when he dusted down an Australian nicknamed the 'Dipper.' He was respectabilised when he became captain and shed the hard-man image, with varying degrees of success. The team manager began calling him 'Michael' to further add to his respectability. Lyons's block-down of Jimmy Kerrigan's goal chance had won the 1987 all-Ireland for Meath, as the ball then went to the other end of the field, and Colm O'Rourke scored a goal. Lyons had a tradition of eating a steak for breakfast on the day of big games. His docker's shoulders and his demeanour gained him respect. His absence cost Meath the 1984 Leinster title. When he wasn't there, as when he was sent off at the end of the second match of Deadlock, it almost cost Meath the match.

Liam Harnan, a first cousin of Lyons, was nicknamed 'Hitman Harnan' after a bone-crunching shoulder on Brian McGilligan in the 1987 all-Ireland semi-final. Meanwhile, his appearance in a television ad, in which he waved a white flag every time John Fenton pucked the ball, added to the glee of colleagues and his own mortification. Boylan likened him to Bertie Cunningham in the 1960s. Meath had not had a presence at centre half-back since.

Padraig Lyons, Mick's brother, was originally the side's penalty-taker. They used to say the ball would end up in the back of the net or else in the swimming-pool in Navan Hospital. He ended up playing in goals for Summerhill.

Kevin Foley was known as the Mario Kempes of the side, probably because his father was born in Argentina. He was a vet, and the team sponsor, Noel Keating, arranged to have him flown by helicopter to football training when he worked in Wexford, Limerick and eventually Cork in his veterinary work. He nearly broke the heart of the man from McElhinney's clothes shop when he wanted to take a trim-and-smart team photograph one all-Ireland morning. He only ever scored once for either club or county, and that was to break the Deadlock.

Terry Ferguson ate more than any normal human, yet he would run the legs off anyone and had less meat on him than on a butcher's knife.

Martin O'Connell was regarded as Meath's most natural footballer, as the best player on the field throughout the Deadlock series and as the most contemporary player to get selected on the Millennium team of 1999. He was slagged by his colleagues for the red hat he wore when he worked in a butcher's in Navan. He began at full-forward in 1986 but eventually became the wing-back of his generation.

Liam Hayes was the sex symbol of the team until the arrival of David Beggy. Now, as captain, he was obsessive about the game and occasionally cranky with his team-mates, including with old friend Colm O'Rourke. He too had a dark childhood secret: the suicide of his brother.

P. J. Gillic came from the townland of Dulane in north

Meath, played minor under-21 and senior the same year and was nicknamed the 'Equaliser' for the physical nature of his play. He turned into a real equaliser when his shot at the end of the first match bounced over the bar.

Colm O'Rourke was nicknamed the 'Professor' and was always complaining that his ankles and knees were not right—with some justification: his career should have ended with a knee injury in 1976. Mick 'Michael' Lyons once gave an entire pre-match talk mimicking O'Rourke's Leitrim accent.

Tommy Dowd, the original third midfielder, was one of the players to emerge in 1991. He was captain in 1996. He eventually lifted the Sam Maguire cup when an outcry over Meath tactics 'had thirty-one counties against us.'

Colm Coyle, small, wiry and hard, featured prominently in 1996, as his last ball bounced, Gillic-style, over the bar to earn Meath a draw with Mayo. He later managed Meath and Monaghan, becoming the first manager in GAA history to resign on a bus, after Meath were defeated by Limerick in 2008.

Brian Stafford was selected for the minor panel but refused to attend training sessions. He was a surprise arrival on the senior panel after the 1986 debacle. In training sessions in Kilmainhamwood he used to bring his dog along to dribble the ball for him. His arrival on the squad was inauspicious: he missed every free he took on the day. Boylan first tried him in a challenge match in Cork; he liked the way he approached the ball and kept him.

David Beggy was regarded by Colm O'Rourke as his one great failure in life ('This is my worst nightmare,' O'Rourke said when Beggy arrived at his first training session on a motorbike), but Beggy's lack of academic focus found other channels: a collection of 800-metre under-age athletics medals. The ban was almost imposed after he sang a few rugby songs on the way to a league match in Co. Mayo, and there was always a sense about him that he was the outsider among GAA men—the man who laughed his way through what was a serious business. He was in the midst of a two-year spell as a legal clerk in Edinburgh at the time of Deadlock, facing a 7:30 a.m. check-in every Monday morning after matches. He was just twenty-eight when his cruciate ligament snapped in a challenge game against Tyrone in 1995, and he never made it back.

Bernard Flynn was renowned as the best dressed on the panel. He once arrived at a match with his gear and a change of clothes for the return journey.

Gerry McEntee, the original 'seventh defender' midfielder, the footballing physician, was noted for the intensity of his approach to football and training. He was married to a Cork woman, and only her lack of interest in football prevented marital strife. He was flown by helicopter from the 1990 all-Ireland final to a transatlantic flight back to his work in Rochester, New York. McEntee was finished the year his one catch had saved Meath against Dublin. In 1991 he re-emerged as a team mentor, then threw off his Sunday suit half way through the third match and decided that he was missing life in the trenches much too much.

Finian Murtagh was the man who introduced the Summerhill and Moynalty lads to the sea when they were running on the dunes in Bettystown.

And Mattie McCabe—the man for whom the number 16 jersey was invented. The Dubs were ready for him to come on and try to score a face-saving goal for Meath in the fourth match of the series. Instead, he made history by telling Kevin Foley to go running up the field.

———

In Dublin—even senior league—if you're fit and you can run with someone and you're reasonably cute, you don't have to be able to kick the ball reasonably well.

—VINNIE MURPHY, March 2003

John O'Leary was the new Paddy Cullen, an inspirational figure who was chosen by Eugene McGee to captain the Irish team against Australia in 1987. His deep voice alone was enough to reassure those around him in the battlefield. He eventually worked with six different Dublin management teams and played seventy consecutive championship games for Dublin.

Gerry Hargan came from Ballymun, where all Dublin's best full-backs were supposed to come from. He made his debut in a November 1982 league match against Kerry, was sent by Heffo to tame Colm O'Rourke in 1983 (occasionally testing the fabric in O'Rourke's shirt) and was still there in 1991, despite his 'need a break from the game' retirement in 1990.

Mick Kennedy had been around since replacing Gay O'Driscoll in the Leinster final of 1979—one of the greatest Dub performances ever and the inspiration for 'The Ballad of the 14 Men.' (Jimmy Keaveney was sent off, and the Pope caused him to miss the all-Ireland final.) He had been caught between two eras, having been on three all-Ireland beaten teams but having missed the 1983 all-Ireland victory because he injured his ankle between the drawn match and replay against Meath. His tussles with Colm O'Rourke were famous.

Tommy Carr was the best-known Dub of all, the soft-spoken captain whose brother Declan played hurling for Tipperary and was to win an all-Ireland medal later in 1991. Tommy's reputation for intensity survived (or was enhanced by) a foul on Brian Murray after just six minutes of the 1993 league final replay, which got him sent off and a six-month suspension, later reduced to four. He went on to manage Dublin, Roscommon and Cavan.

Keith Barr, from Erin's Isle, had been on the Dublin team that beat Meath by sixteen points in the 1986 Leinster minor final, and he earned notoriety when he was sent off for allegedly striking Dinny Allen in the 1989 all-Ireland semi-final.

Eamon Heery began his relationship with Meath by giving Liam Hayes a black eye in the first minute of the 1987 Leinster final. He was the hitman of Dublin, hard as nails, and the raw intensity in his eyes was remembered years later by opponents. His perfectly synchronised shoulder charge with Keith Barr flattened Colm O'Rourke in the fourth match.

Charlie Redmond was the free-taker but, crucially, no longer the penalty-taker. One of his idiosyncrasies was taking a nap in the dressing-room before a match. His free-kick ritual involved licking his gloves three times.

Paul Curran was usually referred to as the 'son of Meath all-Ireland medallist Noel,' and, like many sons of great footballers, he badly wanted to shake the tag off. He played with St Jude's and then Thomas Davis in Tallaght, and he was to become Texaco Player of the Year in 1995.

Niall Guiden, one of two great finds of the 1990/91 league and hero of three matches, reckoned that the way to beat Kevin Foley was to run him into submission. Crucially, and ironically, he went missing when Foley popped up to clinch the goal that ended the Deadlock.

Jack Sheedy, the other find of 1990/91, was making his championship debut against Liam Hayes, with whom he shared a home town.

Paul Bealin, later the midfielder on the 1995 winning team, was to manage Ballyboden to their first Dublin championship and become Wexford and Carlow manager.

Paul Clarke, from Whitehall Colmcilles, was free-taker in

waiting—Barney Rock was also on the bench—to take over from Redmond.

Mick Galvin, from St Oliver Plunketts, was the third full-forward. (Dublin showed a dizzying propensity to switch their forwards around.)

Joe McNally had hung around after his early altercations with Cullen, scoring twice and getting one start and two appearances as a sub. Barney Rock and Ciarán Duff hung around too and were called in for the second match, scoring eight points and a point, respectively. Neither was to get back in favour with the selectors.

Vinnie Murphy was already an iconic figure thanks to his goal-snatching exploits in the league. He later became a financial advisor to a building society. A decade after Deadlock he generated the loudest cheer at Thurles in 2001 when he ran onto the field to play a cameo role in the quarter-final replay between Kerry and Dublin.

———

I believe the audience on Hill 16 were responsible for the deterioration of the game.
—Referee's report, 4 December 1934

The Croke Park of 1991 wasn't designed by anybody. Like the GAA itself it had evolved—a series of largely unplanned accidents: a pavilion in 1910; the tall wall at the railway end in 1915; the rubble pile of rebellion debris that became Hill 16 in 1916; the long stand (originally the covered stand—in reality just a low roof over concrete terracing) in 1922; another stand in 1924 (the new stand or short stand, named for Michael Hogan in 1926); a cycle and athletics track, removed in 1929; a double-deck stand with five thousand seats named for Michael Cusack in 1938; with concrete over Hill 16 in 1936 and concrete over the canal end terracing in 1949; a corner stand (the pensioners' corner—they had a thousand reserved free seats there—named for proxy GAA founder, Pat Nally) in 1952; and another new cantilevered stand, replacing the 1924 and 1918 versions, in 1959. In 1966 seats were installed at ground level under the Cusack Stand, reducing the capacity somewhat.

The issue of crowd management was a haphazard one as the stadium expanded. On occasion, gates at the back of the terracing were forced (as with Kerry v. Armagh in 1953) or crowds were locked out and left without access even to a radio commentary (as in Cavan v. Galway in 1933).

The record attendance for the newly slimmed-down Croke Park was 73,588 at Dublin v. Kerry in 1976, but the capacity afterwards was confined to 69,000. In reality it could have been a whole lot lower.

That was it, as far as the GAA was concerned, until 1983, when a near-disaster at the all-Ireland football final caused a rapid and ill-conceived reconstruction of Hill 16.

Croke Park was a dangerous place in the early 1980s. The fabric of the building hadn't aged well. The seats had been renewed over the decades but still consisted of long planks of wood with concrete arm rests. Reaching the second tier of the stand was a journey through layers of steps.

The area behind the stand had been used for sweet shops, selling pre-packaged sandwiches and cups of hot soup, which were staffed by teenagers from Coláiste Mhuire and Scoil Chaitríona. Throughout the 1970s it was a regular occurrence for crowds to storm the gates at the back of Hill 16 or the canal end, or simply to force them to open them for safety reasons. Entrances and exits were always a challenge, as was getting up or down the mucky slopes at the back of Hill 16 before proper steps were built.

The view could be impeded by a well-placed pillar or

barbed wire, and the crush in exiting the canal end could be rib-puncturing.

The counting process through the turnstiles was accurate enough, but the GAA authorities often added a healthy 12½ per cent cent for children lifted over the turnstiles. An edict to bring this tradition to an end before the 1990 all-Ireland semi-finals was the subject of phone calls to radio chat shows on the unfairness of it all. The GAA said it was the result of an edict from the Government Health and Safety Committee. After the Hillsborough disaster in Sheffield in May 1989, in which ninety-five fans died, stadium events were not what they used to be.

——

It is on Hill 16 that you must feel the Metropolitan ache for glory. An appetite for success that none of the gastronomic delights found in Croker—lonely hot dogs and warm cups of repoured Coke, can satisfy.

—FRANK SHOULDICE, *High Ball,* 1999

One survivor of the Hillsborough reforms was Hill 16. An Bord Pleanála queried the decision to rebuild a piece of stadium architecture where fans were still required to stand on the terraces, but the GAA managed to have the decision overturned. Dubs wanted to stand.

Hill 16 was never a posh place from which to watch the match. That was why it was to there that Dublin fans flocked to celebrate their success of the 1970s. It became a way of satisfying the quest for urban authenticity, for plastic cups of soup—yes, they served 'cup of soup' in the shop at the back—and for much jumping up and down.

Even getting onto the Hill was a rite of passage. It required a few good shoves and an ability to hold your ground; but the initial crush was only a ruse to test out Dub credentials, to keep 'culchies' at bay. Once you made it through the packed denim at the entrance you could always find lots of room at a higher level. You kept moving until you found a view.

———

Bunched in there with your fellow metropolitans it was easy to discern what eau de cologne was all the rage in pre-Celtic Tiger Dubbelin. Hot days, cold days, wet days and, worst of all, damp days, the aroma of 25,000 armpits reaching high to salute each Dublin score. The fan in front of you was always taller and there was such a blizzard of blue flags stretched across the horizon that spotting the ball at all was something of a feat.

—FRANK SHOULDICE, *High Ball,* 1999

When Heffo's Army emerged from the tunnel they raced down to the Hill to claim the end of the neutral ground that was rightfully theirs. There were a few attempts by other teams to steal some psychological advantage: Tyrone in the 1984 all-Ireland semi-final went to the Hill for their kickaround. Unfazed, the Dubs came out and occupied the same spot, while the Tyrone fans in the Hogan sang 'We shall not be moved.' Tyrone paid for their bravado, sinking by 2-11 to 0-8, with Barney Rock personally outscoring them with a tally of 1-7.

The stone toilet behind the goal, long since demolished, was the gathering-point for the most troublesome young supporters.

It was from the Hill that, before the 1975 all-Ireland semi-final, a group of young Dubs began throwing missiles at Derry fans in the Nally Stand. They threw missiles at a small party of GAA officials who walked around the field to see what was happening and then at volunteers pushing fans in wheelchairs behind the goal.

Older Dubs, thronged on the opposite side of the Hill, had enough. Seldom given to chanting, they broke out in an angry chorus, pointing in unison and directing it across the terrace: 'Give it up! Give it up!' The response shocked some of the troublemakers, who then turned on the older crowd.

——

When we're good we're the best in the world, and when we're bad we're the worst in the world.
—DAVE BILLINGS, former manager, talking about Dublin fans

GAA teams in general are pretty dysfunctional families, full of petty jealousies, rivalries, oneupmanships and discords that sometimes date back to trivial events that no spectator at any given game could hope to understand: ancient parish disputes, family feuds and dodgy refereeing decisions dating from a decade or more ago.

With the hopes of a million people resting on their shoulders, and with a complete lack of connectivity between the fans and the club structure, Dublin's GAA family is more fascinating than most—a sort of 'Desperate Househusbands' with their own secret alliances, past crimes and insatiable ambition.

The fans were like no other. One Dublin supporter, from the Thomas Davis club, climbed onto the roof of the Dublin dressing-room and fell through it while Pat O'Neill was giving his half-time team talk at a 1993 championship match at Wexford Park. He landed on the floor, brushed himself off, said sorry and then shouted, 'Up the Dubs!' and walked out.

The fans were an eclectic bunch: good-humoured, faithful and carrying the wisdom brought by being bridesmaids more often than anyone would fancy. Among them also are fans who caused Dublin supporters to be banned from trains, and the man who spat at Tommy Lyons as he left the field after the defeat of 2004, missed, and hit Dave Hendrick on top of the head.

Not many GAA counties do spittle. Dublin's championship prospects are a barometer of city life, of city culture and of how far the GAA has come in bridging that gap between its birthright of green rural fields and the concrete jungles of the shabbier sides of the city.

GAA Dublin isn't Celtic Tiger Dublin. It isn't even the gleaming cathedral of Croke Park, rising to new heights over the inner north side. It's sprawling housing estates where the benefits of the boom never reached; it's the cramped intimacy of Parnell Park and the grim self-evident truth that most summers promise a lot and deliver very little.

Dessie Farrell spoke for every Dublin footballer when he described his recurring nightmare in his biography: he will retire from Dublin and they'll win the very next championship.

It was the same fear that kept the fans coming back.

———

From your standing perch you would see the green swathe of Croke Park, viewing it from an improbable angle of 65 degrees. You'd have to go higher again to clear the ring security fence topped by rolls of rusty barbed wire. It was there to protect normal GAA patrons from us Dubs.

—FRANK SHOULDICE, *High Ball*, 1998

Long before Deadlock the Leinster final of 1984 showed how angry and messy things could be for a GAA follower in the old

Croke Park. A smoke bomb went off and there were crowd invasions and apples thrown.

There were scuffles and occasionally punches thrown between Dublin fans and officials as the entrances to the Nally Stand and the Hogan Stand were closed before throw-in. A side entrance was later opened, allowing fans with tickets to have access to the stands.

Less than ten months earlier things could have been worse. It was a rainy day when the 1983 all-Ireland final was played. A door at the back of Hill 16 was forced, and the GAA was facing its very own Hillsborough disaster. Except it never happened. On the day Hill 16 was reopened for the 1988 all-Ireland hurling, most attention focused on the overcrowding at the canal end, which forced some fans to be accommodated on the other side of the field.

It was clear even to those who ran the GAA that Croke Park would have to be rebuilt.

Chapter 6 ∾

⏐ SEQUENCE OF EVENTS

The precise details of this saga are well recorded in print, on tape and on video. These can never tell the full story.
>   —MICHAEL DELANEY, report to the Leinster
>   Convention, January 1992

Things in Meath were not going well at all. Gerry McEntee, returning to training, found that the mood was really bad in the camp leading up to that first Dublin game. According to McEntee,

> the attitude was awful, and everybody was just fed up. They had had enough and were fighting with each other and were not playing well. Everybody was crabby and there didn't appear to be any real enthusiasm for it at all. Training was bad and things didn't look good. In fact, it looked like Colm O'Rourke and Mick Lyons were going to be dropped. That's how bad things appeared.

O'Rourke had an ankle operation earlier in the year and was finding it very difficult to get right. Pat Reynolds, one of the selectors, rang him the week before the game wondering if the tank had run dry. He assured Reynolds that he was ready to go; but, as he said later, he wasn't really sure, as he was thirty-four years of age 'and had plenty of miles on the clock.' O'Rourke recalled later that, whatever about dropping me . . . it would have been suicide to go out against the Dubs without him. There was an air of menace about Mick and there is no doubt that the Dublin forwards were afraid of him and Liam Harnan. So was I.

A mystery: Meath had two newspaper columnists on their team, and neither of them was talking to the other. Really? Hayes says yes.

Seven days before we first played them in Croke Park, Colm and myself had an almighty row, in the dressing-room. I told him he didn't give a damn about the team and that he should get the feck out of the dressing-room, and stay out. He was less irate, but he still traded words and insisted on having the final say.

Stafford started at number 13, which was foreign to him. 'In the background we knew they were fragile, and we knew we could beat them,' Hayes said.

———

Plan A was to pump everything in high to Vinnie, and, if that wasn't working, Plan B was to pump everything in even higher to Vinnie. In the unlikely event of Plan B failing, we would revert to Plan A.

—CHARLIE REDMOND

Holding the ball. It was Dublin's downfall, or so Paddy Cullen was convinced. He talked of four things: putting fun back into the squad, changing the playing style, releasing the ball earlier and changing the guard. Keith Barr went into Tommy Carr's centre-back position, and Carr went to the wing. Out went Joe McNally, Barney Rock and Ciarán Duff. In came Vinnie Murphy, the long ball and a success in the national league.

Murphy had soared to take the catch and score the goal that won the 1989 Leinster title for Dublin. According to Cullen,

> Vinnie is the kind of player who can win the ball when it's 60-40 against him . . . He is inclined to over-carry. He could not see the need to release the ball early. We thought if we played him full-forward it would reduce the importance of this weakness and play to the strengths: good hands, good feet and very strong.

Kevin Heffernan told Cullen that Dublin were just one or two players away from being a very good side. During the successful national league, confidence in the new direct game was growing. As was confidence in the notion that sharpness was more important than endurance. For Cullen,

> fitness alone is not enough. There is the important matter of doing what you are supposed to do at the time you are supposed to do it, and all in a split second . . . There was a time we put fear into teams. You only do that by winning and winning still more.

The problem with skyscraper passes and big-target football was that everyone in the country knew what Dublin were at by the time the league was won. So when it came to playing Meath, Cullen put David Foran in at number 14 for the first match and Murphy in the corner. Lost their nerve?

Murphy conceded that Foran was that bit older and more experienced, but he objected to his new role.

I think I got a couple of points in the first game, but my confidence was sort of drained at this stage. If he had put me in there and failed that would have been fine; he could have given me twenty minutes.

According to Pat O'Neill,

Dave Foran was a centre-fielder and the reason for putting him at full-forward was his aerial ability and his ability to match someone of the calibre of Mick Lyons man for man. Vinnie was also very good at fielding balls. He had two very good feet. He could concentrate on his main function at corner-forward, which was to win balls and score.

The league final might have decided it. Vinnie Murphy had been gifted a goal against Kildare but was subsequently guarded by John Crofton. It was Keith Barr who won the league for Dublin, not the big full forward. Time for Plan C. McNally was brought back and deemed to be championship-ready after only two nights' training.

_____

It was daunting, because the prospect of being out of the championship in the first week in June was an over-bearing thought.

—COLM O'ROURKE

What was different about 1991? Everything. The rules, the training, the approach, the fact that this was a first round. Only the rivalry was the same.

Tommy Carr felt that both sides were quite tense and nervous about going out of the championship. Jack Sheedy recalled that

> it was more like a league final than a first-round championship game. But there was an intensity to it that I hadn't experienced, at inter-county level, certainly, in the league prior to that.

Charlie Redmond was lying on the bench asleep. He got to the dressing-room an hour and a half before the match to lie down for a kip, a bag behind the head, a towel over his head. Paul Curran used to say, 'We'll wake him up at half time if we need him.' Paddy Cullen didn't like it at all.

> He wanted to see me jumping up, hitting my head off the wall, thumping someone. But that isn't my style at all. Not before the game. I do get exceptionally nervous. I don't show it, but it is inside. I have to get sick in the loo before the game.

Dublin started best. Jack Sheedy hit a half ball into the square, and Robbie O'Malley slid it into the net as Mick Galvin got a hand to it. Dublin led by five at half time. Meath were quite calm in the dressing-room, as Seán Boylan pointed out the problems and set about sorting them out quickly.

The Skryne boys weren't talking to each other for ten days, but they were able to conjure up a penalty. Colm O'Rourke hit a ball in twenty yards from the Dublin goal. In a move himself and Liam Hayes had done a hundred times with Skryne, Hayes just walked in on the blind side and was fouled, and a penalty was given.

> It was almost like automatic pilot . . . He made a great catch thirty yards out, and, typically, four or five

defenders buzzed around him. As they did I sneaked inside them, and Colm flicked the ball over his head. I couldn't believe my luck. I had just John O'Leary to beat, but, as I went to side-step him, somebody nudged my arm, and the ball fell loose. I was about to look for it when Charlie Redmond (bless him), thinking I still had the ball in my arms, hauled me to the ground by the shoulder.

O'Rourke recalled that Brian Stafford

didn't kick it into the net . . . He stroked it into the corner as only he could. His technique off the ground was so perfect that he could have sent over points from all angles and distances while wearing bedroom slippers.

———

Meath, once a great team, sometimes rely on thuggish off-the-ball attacks to make their point. Those players whose assaults are missed by the referee should not get away with thuggery . . . If this means examining videos of matches, or even requesting the gardai to interview players, this should happen.
                                    —'Crack down on GAA thugs,' *Dublin Tribune*

Up in the stand Gerry McEntee and Joe Cassells were watching the game and relaying instructions to the sideline. They berated the veterans, especially Colm O'Rourke and Bernard Flynn, for not giving the ball to the new player, Seán Kelly, who had come back from an injury picked up in the match against Donegal in the league.

When Meath drew level with ten minutes to go, Boylan felt for the first time that they really could have won. Paul

Curran edged Dublin in front again, Dowd equalised, Charlie Redmond put Dublin ahead from a fifty, and Gillic's bouncing ball saved the day for Meath. Seven days to the replay. Gillic recalled that Mick Deegan

> was coming out with the ball down along the Hogan Stand side, and if he had blasted the ball out over the roof of the stand we were probably gone . . . But he chose to solo it out, and Beggy got a great tackle on him. We both went to tackle him at the same time . . . Beggy got there before me, and, as the ball broke, I picked it up . . . I can remember getting around Deegan and going along down the Hogan Stand side and having a look in to see what was going on in the square. I could see Tommy Dowd was bombing it through the middle, and John O'Leary was coming out to cut off the angle . . . I wouldn't say I was going for a point, but I was definitely lobbing it in and hoping something would happen. I was delighted to see it go over, even if initially I was a bit disappointed not to see it drop into the net. But it could have popped wide just as easily.

———

The tie may have been lost in that very first game when Meath recovered from a five-point deficit to draw level.

—JOHN O'LEARY

Meath felt that they had got a draw for playing only twenty minutes' football. The team meeting afterwards was pretty hectic. They hadn't played well, particularly in the first half, and were quite annoyed with themselves. Paddy Cullen, in the immediate aftermath, said that it was

blunder and error, one after the other . . . It was not a
game I enjoyed, not that you can enjoy any game from the
sideline. It was dogged. We played badly, and I wasn't very
happy with it. But if you get out of a game against Meath
and you don't lose, it's a good day.

———

The day football garbage was hung out to dry.
                            —Headline in the *Kerryman*

Physical was what the crowd had come to see. They got what
they wanted: they saw Robbie O'Malley and Mick Galvin
square up to each other, Liam Hayes and David Foran
drawing fists, Mick Lyons clouting Charlie Redmond in
response to an altercation and Liam Harnan whacking
everything that moved.

Galvin suffered a broken jaw and underwent surgery on
Monday night.

Charlie Redmond didn't finish the game—he was
stretchered off. Concussion is now acknowledged as one of
the most serious injuries in the game, and it can have long-
term effects, but the prevailing wisdom at the time (as it was
for a similar incident involving Colm O'Rourke) was that
Redmond would be okay, as his concussion was slight.
Another player commented: 'There were 51,000 people at the
game, and just one person knows precisely what happened to
Charlie Redmond.'

Everyone could name the person, but, in the tradition of
Dublin and Meath football, nobody was not going to
complain after the event. All Redmond would say was that he

collided with someone. There was a great deal of
physicality about the games, and there was a lot of respect

among the players. That respect extended to the fact that, after the game, nobody would whinge in the papers about any moment that happened on the field. If you did you were showing a sign of weakness and nobody wanted to show any weakness.

For Colm O'Rourke, 'all that was good and bad about Gaelic football was in evidence.' According to Jack Sheedy, 'it was physical. It was hard. The pace of the game was very high. It wasn't the greatest game of football played that year.'

The few words of criticism that made their way onto the air waves or into print were confined to the partisan objections to the other team's rough tactics, notably an unsigned opinion piece in the *Dublin Tribune* and one wistful broadside against the general standard of the game, which the former Kerry team masseur Owen McCrohan wrote in the *Kerryman*. McCrohan's piece became a requiem for position play, for high-ball, catch-and-kick football and for a glorious era when Dr Éamonn O'Sullivan from Killorglin was regarded as the guru of the game. He mourned that the

rigid adherence to positional play as advocated by Dr Éamonn has long since been discarded . . . Nowadays we have a tactical game where the emphasis is often shifted from the positive to the destructive. The results are detrimental and there is ample evidence of how far the game has degenerated in recent years.

Much of this latter-day garbage was hung out to dry before 51,000 people at Croke Park last Sunday when Dublin played Meath in the first round of the Leinster championship. What unfolded was an unedifying spectacle devoid of all entertainment value, a free-ridden shambles that proved to be the worst possible advertisement for the code.

Meath and Dublin players have an unhealthy disrespect for each other and it showed in the brutal tackling and the numerous off-the-ball confrontations, all of which went unpunished.

Despite the tension and excitement of the second half, this was largely a forgettable encounter that will hold few cherished memories except for the most partisan supporters of either side. Nobody else could have enjoyed it.

The most bizarre incident of all occurred during the closing sections when Charlie Redmond of Dublin, who played a great game, was floored well away from the action and carried off on a stretcher. Instead of seeking the culprit, the referee blew the final whistle.

———

If players had a better attitude towards the game, a more positive attitude, maybe the rules would not seem so complicated. They should approach the game as a game, not as a duel.

—TOMMY HOWARD interviewed by Tom Humphries, *Irish Times*, 29 June 1991

Tommy Howard was described as an 'up and coming' referee from the Kildare GAA heartlands, a postman and a Kilcullen club man. His progress to the front rank of refereedom hadn't been helped by the presence of another controversial Kildare referee, Séamus Aldridge, who would take priority in big-match appointments throughout the 1970s and 1980s. Howard began refereeing in 1976 at the age of twenty-nine, and at times it seemed that his ambition to referee a match in Croke Park might never be achieved.

He had handled lively and difficult matches in the heated cauldron of the club championship, in all-Ireland finals, Leinster minor finals, Railway Cups and a procession of league matches involving Wicklow, Carlow and other lesser lights, before he was appointed, somewhat surprisingly, to officiate at Dublin v. Meath, next to Cork v. Meath the most heated encounter on the calendar. Until then his biggest appointment had been a Dublin-Armagh league match.

It gave him his big game in Croke Park. In fact he got four of them. The encounters made Howard a household name. The criticism during the first match—all faithfully reported by his wife, Theresa, sitting in the stand—was savage and hurtful. On reflection, Tommy remarked that he had often said the same things about referees himself.

During the series he trained five times a week, doing sprints and running backwards. It wasn't enough. In the third match he got cramp and asked for attention from the Meath physiotherapist. Colm O'Rourke claims that as Tommy Howard was being attended to he was pleading with him to blow it up and let everyone go home. For weeks afterwards Howard had everyone on his route asking if he wanted his leg rubbed.

> Because I am a postman, everyone had a chance during my day to make a comment, so my post route used to take longer than normal. It was all supportive and wishing me the best, but it was on everyone's mind, because there was nothing else talked about at the time for the four weeks.

He even had camera crews down at his house and following him on his route.

Much of the conversation was about how much money he would make for the GAA. Con Houlihan wrote that Howard might be able to trade in his bicycle and buy a nice car. It was a joke, but it wasn't far removed from what was being said around Cam on the canal end terrace. 'It is a ridiculous thought that the referee could go out to have a draw or make a draw out of a match for the sake of making more money for the GAA,' Howard responded.

The Leinster Council didn't have a system of changing the referee for replays. When Tommy Howard's name went in for the first game he was the appointed referee until that saga was finished. The arrangement was based on precedent, not on the rulebook. He was reconfirmed after each match by the council, never knowing in advance that the replay was his. He finished the summer firmly established as the game's best-known referee, having refereed two matches on successive days (on which he refereed the Leinster final and the Down-Kerry all-Ireland semi-final).

Tommy grew with the players. They got to know him. Neither of the counties would have changed the arrangement. After it was all over and the two teams gathered for golf outings, they invited Tommy as well. He was a bit surprised: 'It was only four games of football, after all.' But the party wouldn't be complete without him.

————

Meath and Dublin both have players who will never be candidates for canonisation.

—COLM O'ROURKE

Interest in the encounter hadn't yet reached fever pitch. The Leinster secretary, Michael Delaney, recalls that when the first replay came along he had lots of tickets.

Kevin Moran came back to train with Dublin as a morale-booster the day before the replay. Charlie Redmond broke down in training on the same day. Just before the match Niall Guiden got chickenpox. 'That stuff is contagious,' Paddy Cullen thought. He told Guiden to sit downwind of him—or, better still, in the Meath dugout. It was as good a plan as any.

On the morning of the match the players looked out the window and sighed as one. It was windy, and in Croke Park the wind gives the appearance of blowing from several different directions at once. In the first match it blew directly into the canal goal. In the second it blew directly into the railway goal.

Meath restricted their alterations to some positional changes: Seán Kelly to midfield, P. J. Gillic to full-forward and Tommy Dowd to left half-forward. It was a pattern that was to continue throughout the four matches.

Forces had changed because of the time interval. It was a time for the old stagers, the veterans, to come back in.
—Dublin selector PAT O'NEILL

One of Paddy Cullen's achievements during the league had been to move his side on from the reliance it had had on the survivors of eight years earlier, the 1983 all-Ireland winning team. Ciarán Duff and Barney Rock felt that Cullen and his fellow selectors wanted to be identified by a new-wave Dublin team and that they were the ones to suffer. In the second match the old heads, the discarded players, suddenly found themselves back in favour.

Dublin brought in Donal McCarthy for Guiden and moved Paul Whelan to midfield and Ciarán Duff to left corner-forward.

Into the game came Barney Rock, winning goal-scorer in the 1983 all-Ireland final. His career was so over that he had announced he was standing for the Progressive Democrats in the local elections.

More than anyone else, Rock now required media attention to boost his electoral prospects, and he got his allocation of Sunday sports supplement interviews, some of which questioned his sporting resilience, whether he had ever been the same since Liam Harnan broke his collar bone in the league final of 1986 and whether he could still be as committed, as he was now married and had three young children. The story was simpler than that: his place in the team had been lost through injuries—medial ligaments torn—and a bout of Bell's palsy.

In that second match he scored eight frees and hit the post with what might have been a winner.

The PDS were pleased. It was three weeks to the local elections—historic elections distinguished by the fact that eight councillors who were subsequently found to be involved in controversial land rezonings all lost their seats (including Liam Lawlor), proving that the electorate was well ahead of the legal process, and by the fact that Sadhbh O'Neill, a twenty-year-old student who had done no canvassing and gone to California on a temporary visa, was elected for the Green Party in Donaghmede.

The eight points on the scoreboard wasn't enough for party or player. Rock finished fifth in a race for four Finglas seats, with 940 votes, behind Fianna Fáil's Pat Carey and Tony Taaffe, Fine Gael's Mary Flaherty and the Labour Party's Bill Tormey, and he was overtaken by the Workers' Party candidate, Lucia O'Neill.

The PDS had what they thought was the perfect candidate, and lost. They never parachuted a sporting hero into an election again.

We should have lost the first match; in fact we probably should have lost them all.

—COLM O'ROURKE

Folklore has recorded that the second match was the only one of the four in which Meath had been clearly the better side.

Meath were ahead at half time—the only time this had happened in the series—but Rock's frees ensured that Dublin caught up in the rain-soaked second half.

How many ways might it have ended? With Lyons off the field and Meath's back line disorganised and on the back foot, O'Rourke took a quick free, trying to connect with Terry Ferguson. Ciarán Duff nipped in and intercepted. He lobbed a hopeful ball into the yawning goalmouth gap, where Lyons was no longer available to avert danger. Vinnie Murphy gave Martin O'Connell a neat Séamus Darby-style shove in the back. He turned and shot for goal instead of opting for the point. Mick McQuillan came out quickly and made a brilliant save. From the ensuing mêlée Meath got a free out, which was the last kick of the second match in normal time.

Murphy was aware that it was close enough to the end of the game, but he wasn't aware that it would be the last kick of the game. Later he blamed the frustration from the first game—it had built up. There was a goal on, and he had been presented with the chance he wanted to stick one in to the Dublin management as much as to the Meath men. He says he has nightmares and relives that incident over and over again. But he always returns to the fact that if he had the same chance again he would do the same thing.

It was a natural reaction. That was the feeling that I was having inside. If I got the ball I would have stuck it into the net and won the game.

Vinnie not taking a point in the last ten seconds of the game, Tommy Carr recounted years later, was one of the great disasters of his entire career. He remembered Vinnie and Paul Clarke clashing under the one ball. 'The two of them inside Mick Lyons, and not a sinner in sight,' Carr recalled. The ball popped out of their combined arms directly into Colm Coyle's hands.

> Football immaturity in some circumstances, simply mistakes in others. You'll see it over the championship. Mistakes are the difference between teams winning and losing. Confidence is a huge thing in Gaelic football. That's why Dublin were particularly successful in the 1970s and not in the 1990s, because the individuals they had in the 1970s were confident, mature people who played the game.

> ——

> Out of the four games we would have said we should have won three of them. Coming out of the second game we would have said we are a little fortunate today, we didn't play as well as we did the first day, we didn't dominate Meath as much as we did the first day, and we were happy enough to end up in the changing-room with the draw at that stage.
>
> —PADDY CULLEN

Now there was a procedural matter to be cleared up. Mick Lyons had been sent off a couple of minutes before the end of the match. Because extra time was constituted as a new game, Seán Boylan felt that he could be substituted. Tommy Howard disagreed. Liam Creavin had to go across to the referee's room and consult with whatever council members could be found, who indicated that Meath could bring on a sub. On came Liam Harnan.

Mick Lyons sent off? Seán Boylan claims that Lyons had a reputation he didn't deserve.

> To hear people talking you'd think he was put off every Sunday. The first time was for a personal foul against Roscommon; the second was for the third of the four-in-a-row matches against Dublin. The TV replays showed he wasn't within yards of the player. He was nearly getting blamed for not having hit the fellow. He never said anything; he just turned around and walked off.

Meath were not the only beneficiaries of the 'new game' rule. Donal McCarthy of Dublin, who had been booked in normal time, was booked again in extra time, when he might have been sent off.

In the second minute of extra time Bernard Flynn's well-directed pass gave David Beggy a yard of space. He jinked around the defender and, as O'Leary advanced, put it into the unguarded top corner. Did O'Leary get his hand to it? Beggy said no. Meath were three ahead when Rock's long kick was punched into the goal by Jack Sheedy. Three players from each team were booked. Donal McCarthy had the distinction of being booked twice, the second time in extra time, which was admissible under the rules.

When Colm O'Rourke wrote that David Beggy trapped his foot when he was about to shoot late in the game, his team-mates said it was 'to prevent another wide.' Such devotion to duty.

Tommy Howard blew the whistle twenty seconds early with an almost theatrical gesture of relief. A fortnight to the next replay.

Four cramps to nil means nothing.

BERNARD FLYNN

Cramp was the word. The players were not wearing well. In the last twenty minutes of extra time in the second match neither team was able to score, and they created only two reasonable chances between them.

When four Dublin players went down with cramp, and none for Meath, questions were asked about Dublin's training. 'This was one of the fittest teams in Ireland, and like flies they went down with cramp,' Seán Boylan commented. 'Uncle Seán's weed-killer was obviously doing its trick for us,' Colm O'Rourke said afterwards.

In 1990 David Foran had Dublin's training, geared towards 120-minute games, stepped up to five or six sessions just before the Leinster final. His worries were far from Paddy Cullen's. The consensus after Colm O'Rourke's goal dumped Dublin from the championship was that they had over-trained. So in 1991 Cullen adopted a different approach. Dublin trained at Parnell Park on Tuesday and Thursday nights and on Saturday mornings, much like they had done in the 1970s. Foran kept training sessions to the duration of a normal match, aware that he had to have the players at their peak for the latter stages of the championship, as well as for that unprecedented first round against Meath.

According to Pat O'Neill, Dublin's training at the time was essentially speed training. He explained the cramps by saying that the team got caught with two heavy games in seven days and extra time. Dublin's players consumed ten litres of water and six litres of saline and glucose, and the bench ran out of both in the last fifteen minutes.

Boylan's trademark Meath training since 1983 had been based on endurance. They generally trained on Tuesday and Thursday nights, with Saturday and Sunday mornings

John O'Leary and Bernard Flynn shaking hands after the first of four matches. The friendship among the players developed over the years, reinforced by golf-day reunions modelled on the outings enjoyed by Dublin and Kerry rivals of the 1970s. (© *Ray McManus/ Sportsfile*)

Tommy Carr and Colm O'Rourke were household names before the Deadlock series and were to become key interpreters of events. Carr was Dublin's on-field leader and tactician who later went on to manage the county team. Colm O'Rourke was a supporter of Boylan and effectually a proxy manager from the mid-1980s, helping to stave off Boylan's county board critics during difficult times. He inspired the Meath attack from the centre-half-forward position. (© *Ray McManus/Sportsfile*)

Mick Galvin celebrates a goal during the first match in the Deadlock series. He suffered a broken jaw in the match but returned to score again in the fourth encounter. (© *INPHO*)

Jack Sheedy's goal, cancelling out a three-point lead for Meath, was a key moment of the second match. Thereafter it was Meath who tended to chase Dublin's lead. (© *INPHO*)

The aftermath. (© *INPHO*)

Referee Tommy Howard blows for a foul on Colm O'Rourke by Keith Barr and Paul Bealin. O'Rourke spent much of the fourth match suffering from concussion after his increasingly rough handling by his markers. (© *INPHO*)

David Beggy was to become part of the legend of Deadlock for his winning point in the fourth match. His arrival on the Meath panel added marketability and excitement to what was a highly traditional squad set-up. Before his winning point in 1991 his most famous accolade was having been to Croke Park only once, for a U2 concert, before he played there for the first time. (© *David Maher / Sportsfile*)

Paddy Cullen and Seán Boylan shake hands after Deadlock had ended. Both managers had been chosen with a clear task in mind: Boylan's was to restore stability and credibility to Meath football, which appeared to have lost its way at the end of the 1970s. He did this through a longevity that was to be as legendary as his achievements. Cullen was brought in to restore much-needed 1970s glamour to Dublin's burgeoning but under-achieving football culture. The result of the Deadlock series had a key part in the reputations of both managers and their teams that was to endure long into the decade: Meath became associated with resilience in adversity and Dublin with fragility. (© *INPHO*/*James Meehan*)

Unlikely goal-scorer, unlikely hero, Kevin Foley's fame rested uneasily on his shy shoulders. Parents named their sons in his honour after his equalising goal in the fourth match of the Deadlock series. (© *INPHO*)

Keith Barr was selected to take Dublin's penalty in the fourth match of Deadlock because his kick was regarded as stronger than the usual 1988–90 penalty-taker, Charlie Redmond. Barr was to claim that he was distracted by Mick Lyons, who chose to run alongside him as he approached the ball as a diversionary tactic. Barr kicked powerfully as planned but sent the ball wide. Nevertheless the penalty should have been retaken because of Lyons's interference. (© *Ray McManus/Sportsfile*)

(© *Billy Stickland/*INPHO)

Meath score a point, with an unresponsive Hill 16 in the background. Much of the drama in the fourth and final match of Deadlock was to unravel below the theatrical blue backdrop of the Hill, often reflecting the blue summer sky and bringing a bucolic mirror lake feel to north-side inner-city Dublin. (© *Sportsfile*)

Ireland's most famous postman, Tommy Howard, throws the ball in among the four midfielders to restart the match, Paul Bealin, Liam Hayes and P. J. Gillic among them. The ritual of the throw-in, enacted twelve times over the series, was to become a battle within a battle, with its own unique set of tactics and anticipatory moves. (© *INPHO*)

P. J. Gillic celebrates with Ian Kearney at the end of the Deadlock series, having played a key part in the final act of the drama. Gillic's bouncing ball had gone over the bar to save the first match for Meath. At the end of the fourth match he supplied the pass for David Beggy for the Meath winning point. It was a remarkable cyclical endgame. Beggy in turn had helped make the bounced point that created the Deadlock in the first place. (© *James Meehan/INPHO*)

Tommy Carr attempts to block Dave Beggy's shot. Much of the mythology of Beggy's inability to score was born of his unpredictable and unorthodox style; in fact he had been a relatively consistent scorer for Meath down the years. (© *INPHO*)

Keith Barr and Robbie O'Malley jump for possession. The style of football played by Dublin and Meath was sometimes blamed for bringing an end to the classic high-fielding game beloved of the middle-aged GAA legislators. The 1991 rules were designed to curtail the close-marking possession-minded style of the teams. Ironically, the first high-profile games under the new rules were to result in the four-match Deadlock series between Dublin and Meath. (© *INPHO*)

Croke Park in 1991 was an aged and shabby stadium, built in three waves of 'concrete-mixer' investment in 1938 and 1959 and an ill-conceived reconstruction of Hill 16 in 1988. The funds and profile generated by the Deadlock series gave the GAA the confidence to redevelop the stadium by 2003 into Europe's third-largest stadium, fitted out with all the conveniences of the best international sports arenas. (© *INPHO*)

Paul Bealin and Liam Hayes in action in one of the key dramas within the greater drama of the Deadlock series. Curtailing the expansive Hayes style was to be a problem for all Meath's opponents in the 1980s and 90s. (© *David Maher/Sportsfile*)

Mick Lyons in action against Vinny Murphy, whose moves between corner-forward and full-forward reflected the Dublin management's anxiety about whether their 'high ball to Vinny' approach could work with the famously aggressive Meath full-back. In fact Lyons's sending off during the Deadlock series was only the second in his career. (© *Ray McManus/Sportsfile*)

Niall Guiden and Colm Coyle in action. The strict zonal man-marking system used in Gaelic football meant that opponents got to know each other too well in a series of replayed matches, often with all-too-predictable results. (© *Ray McManus/ Sportsfile*)

thrown in, often on Bettystown beach and then in Dalgan Park, near Navan.

After a spell of hard sessions in the spring, Meath concentrated on football during the summer months. The training programme was all based on skill-development, although Boylan and others nurtured the idea that it was based on raw power throughout the year.

In 1991, however, he was 'concerned about the mileage on some of the clocks' and about the catalogue of injuries the team were facing.

He was interested in how Joan Benoit, an American athlete, had used water-training to win the marathon gold medal at the 1984 Olympics almost immediately after undergoing arthroscopic surgery on her knee, and only two years after surgery for an injury to her Achilles tendon. He decided to move the team's stamina-training offshore—or at least to the waters of Gormanston College swimming-pool.

With the help of the middle-distance runners Gerry O'Reilly and Sonia O'Sullivan he obtained buoyancy aids from Glenn McWalter in the United States for the players. He hadn't anticipated the cost—£3,000 or the fact that some of the players couldn't swim. That was the stamina-training before Deadlock. 'It saved my career and got a few more years out of many others whose joints were a bit ropey,' O'Rourke wrote. They eventually did their first work on the field three weeks before the first match.

Four Dubs got cramp in extra time. Those evenings in the wetsuits meant that Meath stayed on their feet.

Dublin also had a diet regime for their players, but, as Pat O'Neill said, 'we had a compliancy problem.'

———

There is no enjoyment about of any of this. It has become more of a chore than anything else. It's extremely hard work.

—DAVID BEGGY after the third match

The Leinster Council fixed a date for the fourth match even before the third had taken place—just in case. They set it for Saturday 29 June. The Leinster hurling semi-finals, by now a secondary event, were postponed from 23 June to the 30th.

It was at this point that interest in the fixture became abnormal. Tickets were now in demand. For tickets for the second and third replays there was chaos, with only four people working in the Leinster Council office in Portlaoise trying to get out sixty thousand tickets.

Michael Delaney, the secretary, recalls that a friend of Brian Mullins rang him and asked to bring forty clients to the first match and to dinner. He didn't want to spend more money but repeated the arrangement for the four games. By the time it came to the fourth game it was getting tougher to get decent Hogan Stand tickets.

This difficulty extended to the participants. For the first match, players got only two tickets each, allocated on the Saturday night, one from the Leinster Council and one from their county board. On the second week it went up to four tickets. But that was about as good as it got for the men who generated £1,111,898 for the GAA.

The organisers soon found that they were unexpectedly running out of programmes. Dubliners are notoriously bad programme-buyers. The policy for all-Ireland finals is to print one programme for every two spectators, and for Leinster championship matches to print one programme for every three spectators. When the Dubs are playing, the Leinster Council reduces it to one programme for every five spectators. It was clear by the third match that this was no longer enough, as all the programmes were sold out half an hour before throw-in.

———

> Heart and wit, and not a lot else, carried Meath along from week to week. Until Dublin suddenly, inexplicably slowed up with the finishing-line in sight, on 6 July.
>
> —MICK MCQUILLAN

Back to the old ways. In the 1970s Tony Hanahoe would move around the field, opening up the middle for his team-mates. Jack Sheedy was to do the same, sacrificing his game for the sake of the team and moving to benign parts of the field, taking Liam Harnan with him and taking the hit man out of the game. It didn't work. The players surrounding Sheedy were not like those surrounding Hanahoe. Harnan wasn't for moving either. By the third game the Dublin selectors had had enough. They kept Sheedy *in situ.*

The third match was played on a wet, misty day. Often on wet days in Croke Park whoever gets a lead doesn't lose it— but again it finished in a draw.

The players were slipping all over the place, but the match was later regarded as the best of the series. Meath reeled Dublin back from a five-point lead in the final eight minutes. Bernard Flynn scored a goal in the sixty-second minute, when he fisted a ball past goalkeeper John O'Leary from Colm Coyle's bending cross. According to Flynn,

> for fifteen or twenty minutes we were absolutely blown away by Dublin's pace . . . They were running at us, particularly in defence; they were causing trouble, getting frees. With about 13 minutes to go it did look ominous. Meath looked in serious trouble . . . At the team meetings

over the years we spoke about John's liking for coming off his line. Down the years Meath would have got a few scores from it. Colm Coyle was going for a score, but it dropped short. It was sneaking in behind Mick Deegan. I slid across John O'Leary's body, and I got a hand in ahead of it.

Stafford, having sent a fifty wide, kicked a point from play and then got the free that might send the match into extra time once more. He said a prayer before he kicked it. It went over, to the thunderous cheers of the Meath supporters.

———

Forget the opening seventy minutes and go straight to extra time.

—RTE commentator MICK O'DWYER

Jack Sheedy noticed something different happening in the third match.

As a forward you were further away from the main group of players, and the handshakes were different. The players were looking at each other in a different way, a 'we are all in this together' sort of thing; we don't know really what it is, but we are in it together.

For Tommy Carr,

you couldn't see yourself either winning or losing . . . It just seemed to be starting to go on for ever. The same faces. The same half-time talks. The same post-mortems at the end of the games. You would have a pep-talk before, in the middle of half time, before extra time, in the middle of extra time. It just seemed to go on and on.

As Dublin captain, Carr had his speeches ready for any eventuality. Before the first game he gathered his players in a huddle and said, 'This is it, lads, our big game against Meath. This is the one we must win.'

At half time the players gathered around the captain. 'Just thirty-five minutes left, lads—the last thirty-five minutes against Meath. This is it.'

Minutes before the start of the replay: 'Okay, lads, this is our very last match against Meath.'

At half time in the replay: 'We can do it now, lads, we can finish them off.'

Just before extra time: 'This is it, lads—the last act.'

By half time in extra time he had run out of words. There he was, standing in the middle of the players, feeling that they expected him to say something profound. He began, 'What can I say, lads?'

Eamon Heery replied, 'Say feckin' nothing.'

———

I wonder if they have thought of this little snag: another draw after extra time in the replay. One day it will happen in a crowded fixtures programme and there is no provision in the rules for a soccer type shot out or other sudden death resolution.

—PADDY DOWNEY, before the third match, *Irish Times*,
5 June 1991

Because of the 'new game' rule, discovered accidentally by means of the Mick Lyons incident in the second match, Dublin had a new trick up their sleeve. They brought on two players at the start of extra time who wouldn't now be counted as substitutes: Ray Holland and Charlie Redmond.

Extra time was only fourteen seconds old when Colm Coyle, who had moved into the right corner of the attack at the railway end, snatched a Meath goal. John O'Leary missed a centre from substitute Gerry McEntee. The tendency for O'Leary to move out of his goal had been noticed by Meath, and Coyle was alert to the opportunity. Dublin kept their nerve and responded with a goal from Paul Clarke three minutes later to send the noise from the crowd a notch higher. For anyone who wished to sample the passion of the entire four afternoons of Deadlock at its greatest, all they had to do was to sit through this short segment of play.

Keith Barr had a late tackle on Colm O'Rourke. Tommy Howard had to go looking around all the Dublin full-back and half-back line to find the culprit. According to Howard, who was criticised for taking so long to find Barr,

> it got to the stage that I knew all the players personally. It wasn't a question of what number or anything; I just had to find him. Keith, he sort of disappeared into the crowd, as it were, but I was determined to have a word with him, and I found him on the goal-line.

Paul Curran scored the equalising point: 'Tommy Dowd slipped and fell, which gave me an about ten yards' advantage. There wasn't anybody looking for the pass, so I just went for the point. That was it.'

For Seán Boylan, 'this was a mix of all that is great and all that is stupid in Gaelic football.' When asked in the dressing-room about the decision to select Gerry McEntee for the third match, Boylan just responded, 'It wasn't a mistake.' Paddy Cullen was still joking. 'We like to make a few bob for the Association.'

The front page of the *Irish Press* on Monday was entirely

devoted to Meath and Dublin. A slim strip in black across the bottom of the page whispered: 'Shocks for big parties in latest opinion poll, See page 2.'

The foresight of the Leinster Council meant that there was a fortnight's break between the third and fourth matches. Dublin headed back to Parnell Park; Meath headed for Scotland.

———

I would worry that they would come back mentally exhausted.
——DR AIDAN MORAN on Meath's decision to go to Scotland
between the third and fourth matches, *Irish Independent*,
28 June 1991

After the second match of Deadlock the Meath chairman, Fintan Ginnitty, asked Seán Boylan if he wanted to take the team away on a break. Boylan turned the offer down, but by the time they were preparing for the fourth match he was reconsidering. 'There was no escape from the mounting tension and hype at home, and it was crucial to get away,' Boylan said later.

He flew over to see David Beggy, who was working in Scotland, and Beggy drove him and the CEO of Kepak, Noel Keating, to the Buchanan Arms Hotel, a 52-bed former coaching inn in Drymen, half way between Glasgow and Stirling, on the bonny banks of Loch Lomond. The town is best known as the setting for Billy Connolly's birthday parties, and the weekend Boylan organised there at short notice for players and partners was Connollyesque in its extremes.

Drymen was full of wetmen—extremely wet Meathmen—for the weekend. 'We did some training over there but mostly tried to drink the place dry,' Brian Stafford recalled. The wet nights were followed by four-hour training sessions on a local soccer pitch.

'It was a major logistical problem to get them all there,' Boylan said, 'and it cost a small fortune; but then we were lucky to have a generous sponsor who came with us.' Colm O'Rourke noted that the preparation

> would not be found in any training manual . . . We arrived on Friday evening and got straight down to business in the bar. By the end of the night we were so stupid we even thought we could sing and started karaoke. The bar ran out of drink. Next day they ran out of water as we paid the price with a heavy training session. But we all relaxed, let off steam and were ready to go again . . . On the Thursday night at training the players were told to have everything ready for the following morning. Wives, children, babysitters were to be sorted; we were to be at a certain place at a certain time, and they were going away. They didn't even know where we were going until they reached the airport, and wives and girlfriends were brought too. The girls got five-star treatment while the fellows were training.

According to Kevin Foley, Boylan 'left a lot of the football to the people on the pitch . . . Getting them in the right frame of mind going out was what he was mostly focused on. It's probably the most important thing, at the end of the day.'

One session of seventy minutes was spent running up and down the field, passing the ball and building up long sequences of passes, and Foley was one of the lads who featured in every move. Liam Hayes recalls that Scotland was

> a defining period for the team, almost like the team was

going away to make peace with itself and have its last official going-away party . . . We were a group that had been together a long time. We knew each other very well. We had fallen out a lot. We had made up a lot . . . We partied hard in Scotland and drank long into the night, and trained hard. And the team defined itself after that.

Others were not so sure. The flood of psychologists into the back-room teams of GAA counties that followed Derry's success in 1993 was still two years off.

In 1991 the GAA was psychoanalysed for the first time. The sports psychologist Aidan Moran of UCD said that Meath

may come back physically refreshed, but because they are having a compete break from football they will put the match out of their minds. Then on return they will have to psych themselves up again and they will see this as something difficult and unpleasant that they are coming back to. That usually makes motivation much harder.

He still expected Meath to win, 'because marathon encounters have a greater toll on teams that are trying to prove themselves.'

He said that because of their age and the amount of chopping and changing in Dublin's line-up their players would have less self confidence.

———

I went up and I struck the ball. I struck it to Mickey Quinlan's right-hand side. I thought I struck the ball well, but unfortunately I didn't put it on target. It was a miss—it was a critical miss.

—KEITH BARR

While the Meathmen were running up and down the field in Drymen, Keith Barr was practising penalties. He had a ferocious kick. 'We practised and practised,' Pat O'Neill said. 'It's a pity we didn't get better results.'

———

> Imagine spending the rest of one's days reporting replays of this first round game. It is most unlikely that the deadlock would continue but if it should happen what would the Leinster Council do to break it? Would the GAA be forced to call a special Congress?
>
> —PADDY DOWNEY, *Irish Times*, 19 June 1991

The Deadlock was broken in normal time in the fourth match. The teams had been through the four seasons in three weeks. The weather had been cold, wet and drizzly; and now, for the last game, the sun shone on a beautiful day, the blue of the July sky reflecting the blue on Hill 16.

The drama of the fourth day began even before the throw-in. Seán Kelly failed a fitness test the day before the match. As Terry Ferguson took off his trousers he jerked his back and was in so much pain he couldn't move. That freak accident led to a lifetime of back trouble and a disc operation. Padraig Lyons came on for Terry, but fifteen minutes into the match his hamstring went—he never played for Meath again. After five minutes Colm O'Rourke was sandwiched between Keith Barr and Eamon Heery and was carried off concussed. Paddy Cullen heard the crunch.

> It was a heart-stopping moment. At first I thought he was badly injured. Then my second thought, when he wasn't dead, was that maybe now we had a chance.

The Meath doctor, Jack Finn, cleared all the substitutes off the bench to allow O'Rourke to lie down flat until he came round and could be sent back into battle.

Seán Boylan was going to replace him, but Jack kept saying, 'No, give him a minute, he's coming to.' Keith Barr, who was playing centre half-back, had nobody to mark. He had five or six minutes to go up the field and punish Meath, but he didn't. For ten minutes after he resumed O'Rourke didn't know where he was.

Legend has it that Barr and Heery apologised to O'Rourke afterwards and said that he would probably have done the same to them. 'With one difference,' he replied. 'You wouldn't have got up again.'

O'Rourke referred to the incident in his memoirs. 'Even with all the hard men I have played against there are none who wished to do serious damage to an opponent. A good hard wallop is okay, but nothing that would stop a person going to work the following day.'

I have never experienced such tension in the build-up to any match as that fourth game; it was bigger than the all-Irelands.

—COLM O'ROURKE

Dublin led by two points at half time and stretched the lead to six points in the second half. 'The first time Dublin played with real flair,' O'Rourke felt.

Boylan was unperturbed even as Dublin were in the process of shooting five points without interruption. When Keith Barr sauntered forward and scored a point he turned to Pat Reynolds and said, 'We're grand now; once a half-back scores he will want to score more, and lose focus.'

Focus was now the issue. Jack Sheedy felt that Dublin were getting scores a lot easier than in any of the previous games. 'It just seemed we were moving forward; we were getting our scores. I began to feel that if we could keep this going and don't make any silly mistakes we just might get over the hump.'

Eleven minutes into the second half Meath's most famous sub, Mattie McCabe, came on for Bernard Flynn, who had an injured calf muscle. Both were to have a hand in the breaking of Deadlock: McCabe for something he said to Kevin Foley, and Flynn for his absence—for not being in position to the right of P. J. Gillic to accept the ball before the winning point. If Gillic knew it was Beggy, not Flynn, that was to his right he might never have made the pass.

Forced to watch the final twenty-four minutes from the bench, Flynn felt that the three matches and the history between the teams over the previous five years were what cost Dublin their victory. 'They were looking over their shoulder a little bit.' Hayes, as always, felt that Dublin were fragile.

The most amazing thing, really, was the calmness of our team. Even during the second half, when the game looked lost, there was never any stage of panic. There was never any stage . . . when we felt the game was over. None whatsoever. They thought they had the game won. They certainly thought they had the game won, and you could feel that on the field. They started loosening up a little bit. The game, because they were quite dominant, began to break up a little bit, became a bit frayed around the edges.

———

In the end what happens on the field is a reflection of many many things, most of which we can't see from the sideline.

—EAMON DUNPHY, *Sunday Independent,* 7 July 1991

O'Rourke, apparently no longer concussed, signalled his return by sending the pass to Brian Stafford for a Meath goal in the fifty-second minute. Dublin responded by stretching the lead to four, before Stafford cut the lead to three points with eleven minutes to go.

> We won a free on the Cusack side, shooting to the Hill on the 20-metre line. I was kind of half-reluctant to take it but went over to kick it anyway. It was probably the hardest free-kick I ever took in Croke Park.

Eight minutes from the end Declan Sheehan was fouled, and Dublin were awarded a penalty. Out on the sideline Seán Boylan was shouting at Hayes, 'Even if they score we can still win,' and telling him that the team should 'throw the ball around like you did in Scotland.'

———

> Do the Dubs have a penalty clause in their contract?
> —JOE DUFFY jibes the Dublin forwards on RTE radio, 1992

Scoring a penalty was a problem for four generations of Gaelic footballers.

The task was more difficult than it should have been. The original football penalty, under the 1945 rules, was kicked from 14 yards (later changed to 13 metres) into a target of 168 square feet. It wasn't until 2010 that this was shortened to 11 metres. Soccer penalties are taken from 12 yards into a target area of 192 square feet.

Of the penalties awarded in the championship during the 1990s, only 53 per cent were scored. It presented a neat incentive for a defender, considering that one in two penalties was missed.

Dublin had the worst record of all from the penalty spot, scoring only one goal (Charlie Redmond v. Kildare in 1994) from eight attempts in the championship between 1988 and 2000.

One of their famous misses was before Deadlock: the 1988 Leinster final against Meath, in which Charlie Redmond put the last kick of the match over the bar when a goal was needed for a draw. Another three famous misses were after Deadlock: the 1992 all-Ireland final against Donegal, when Redmond missed early in a match that Dublin were leading but eventually lost; the 1994 all-Ireland final against Down, when Redmond missed in the final quarter with Dublin trailing; and the 1997 Leinster first-round match against Meath, when Paul Bealin hit the bar with the last kick of a match in which Dublin were trailing by three points.

And so, in the sixty-second minute of the fourth match of Deadlock, into that great Dublin catalogue of calamity—the missed list—stepped Keith Barr.

———

I honestly didn't notice Mick Lyons at the time. I know he's a hard man to miss, but I was just so focused on the ball. Unfortunately I beat Mickey McQuillan but the post beat me on the day.

—KEITH BARR

The reason that Keith Barr was the penalty-taker rather than the 1988–90 taker, Charlie Redmond, was that he had such a powerful kick. Pat O'Neill says, 'In our management time it was always practised. It's disappointing that we didn't have a good result despite all the time we put into penalties.'

It was almost the perfect penalty. The shot travelled with such force that it dislodged the flag at the side of the goalpost. The Meath goalkeeper, Mick McQuillan, later described it as the best penalty taken against him. 'It was hard and low, and I have not seen many better penalties, but thankfully it went wide. Even if I had got a hand to it, the ball would have gone back out to him, and he probably would have scored.'

Everyone in attendance—except the referee—had seen Mick Lyons run alongside him as the kick was being taken. Meath players joked afterwards: 'Keith beat Mick in the run to the ball.' On the fifteenth anniversary DVD, *Battle Royal,* Charlie Redmond recalls Tommy Howard looking at Keith kicking the ball, with Mick Lyons standing between them. 'How Tommy didn't tell him to retake the penalty, I'm completely amazed, because he's not looking at the goal; he's looking at Keith, and Mick Lyons is in his way.'

Tommy Howard said that 'technically it should have been retaken . . . but as I spoke to Keith Barr afterwards he said he hadn't even seen anyone running with him. He said it was just a badly taken penalty.'

——

Dublin are playing so well at the moment that I don't think it will make any difference. They're winning all over the pitch.
—RTE commentator MICK O'DWYER, after Tommy Carr went off injured in the third match

With four minutes to go, Meath looked well and truly buried. Paddy Cullen thought so to himself on the Dublin bench. Liam Hayes recalled: 'We looked disorganised, and every one of us felt disheartened.' As Vinnie Murphy came on for Charlie Redmond in the sixty-sixth minute the two players high-fived each other. They thought the game was won—the first time they had thought so throughout the entire series. Meath saw the two Dubs high-fiving and decided to dig deep. Tommy Carr was called to shore, leaving one of the Dublin selectors to mourn later that 'when he went off, the proverbial hit the fan; we had no anchor to halt the slide.' Redmond recalled: 'We fell asleep in those last two or three minutes, and we let Meath back into the game.'

The Meath men thought of Scotland, of the hand-passing movements up and down the tiny pitch in Drymen. 'Everyone was showing for that last move,' Bernard Flynn recalled. 'It was clinical. It was like the last hurrah.'

Three minutes remaining. Dublin 0-15, Meath 1-9. Tommy Carr recalled:

> We were all moved around . . . Because Seán Boylan was moving his players around, sometimes we stuck in a position, sometimes we moved with the player. In terms of the structure and its methodology of the game, everything went out the window in the last game, especially in the second half.

Kevin Foley saw the stewards circling the field for the end of the match. He wasn't having the best spell of a game in his career. His man, Niall Guiden, had just kicked over what were to be Dublin's last two points of the encounter.

In the absence of any other ideas, he was moving forward, crossing midfield without Guiden, or indeed anyone else, noticing him. His team-mates were to remark that once he got over the half-way line he was lost, in a different world altogether.

Mattie McCabe, a man who knew something about scoring goals against Dublin—he scored in each of the Leinster finals: 1987, 1988 and 1989—saw him and said, 'I'll go back, you keep going. Nobody will follow you, but if I go and get involved they will follow me.' Kevin went. Nobody followed. Once he was past the half-way line the voice took over. Destiny guided him to a certain place at a certain time. History was waiting for him four yards in front of the Hill 16 goal.

––––

It should be used as an example to kids around the country who are being taught the game. It was the perfect example of teamwork and support play, and what started off at the back ultimately ended up in a goal. It was the perfect goal.

—CORMAC SULLIVAN

There are moments in football history when there has been a well-worked double-feint team move, a sleight of hand or foot—when a man who seemed to be rambling carelessly out of position wasn't followed, when someone moved out of position just long enough to score a crucial goal.

Séamus Darby's was the most famous of these. A half-forward was replaced by a substitute who, instead of taking up the half-forward position, had been told to move to corner-forward. A half-back had to follow him into the unfamiliar corner position, and, in the moment of hesitation or confusion, history turned. Darby nudged and out-jumped Doyle and scored the goal.

This is what happened to Kevin Foley at 5:24 p.m. on 6 July 1991.

––––

Unbelievable.

—MICHEÁL Ó MUIRCHEARTAIGH

Seagulls like Croke Park. They especially like to congregate on the roof of the old Cusack Stand over the railway goal. That's where the drama was about to unfold.

Eleven passes leading to Foley's goal. The most famous eleven passes in football history: O'Connell, Lyons, McCabe, Harnan, O'Rourke, Beggy, Foley, Gillic, Dowd, O'Rourke, Dowd.

————

> In Scotland we did nothing but move up and down the field, for seventy minutes, non-stop. The type of move at the end of the match that led to the famous Kevin Foley goal that was started in the corner—we practised those moves, and it proves the more you practise the better you get.
>
> —SEÁN BOYLAN

The move started with Vinnie Murphy, newly arrived on the field, giving away a bad pass and Martin O'Connell preventing the ball going out of play—just about—at the canal end. O'Connell famously claimed afterwards that as he did so his left boot crossed over the end line and that the move might never have happened. Another player would have let it roll over the end line and leave it for the goalkeeper to kick downfield.

Dublin sensed what Meath were attempting. Mick Lyons to Mattie McCabe to Liam Harnan. When Harnan linked with O'Rourke at the half-way point, Mick Kennedy did what every self-respecting Dublin defender of the 1980s would have done: he fouled O'Rourke. Man and ball, one and all.

The next part was Tony Hanahoe's fault. The eleven passes included a break in play that before the Hanahoe rules would have been enough to bring the entire movement to a halt.

The Hanahoe rules allowed the free kick to be taken quickly.

A year earlier the movement would have ended there and then. The ball would have been placed, defenders would have regrouped and there would have been no goal. The changed rules allowed O'Rourke to jump to his feet and poke a short free from his hands to David Beggy. Dublin's defenders were not given the time to reorganise.

———

The number-one rule in the handbook of every Meath footballer, as written by Seán Boylan, is to score more goals than Dublin, and victory is almost assured.

—TOMMY DOWD

O'Rourke's quick free wasn't the straightest of kicks. On another day it might even have gone directly over the sideline.

When he got it Beggy didn't seem to know what to do with it at first. He sent it to Kevin Foley, who wasn't moving at all. Foley passed to Tommy Dowd and started to move again.

Dowd gave it to O'Rourke, and he gave it back to Dowd. 'I didn't think he would,' Dowd recalls. 'I thought he'd turn around and blast it himself. But he did.' Foley was to tell Colm O'Rourke later that 'you were obviously still concussed or you wouldn't have returned the pass to Tommy Dowd.'

Dowd saw John O'Leary coming for him.

I would never take a shot at John O'Leary if I was ever in that sort of position. I would either try and give it to a man outside who was in front of the goal or try and get round him . . . I would never try and take a shot, because he was such a good shot-stopper. I didn't even know who was outside me at the time. I just saw a green jersey, and

Kevin Foley happened to be there in that position. It could have been Stafford for all I knew at the time.

As Foley tried to shoot, John O'Leary tried to scramble across goal to block. He missed it by a fingernail.

Fair play to him; he was brave enough to keep going. A lot of lads when they made the pass would have run back down into the defence to pick up a man, but he kept going. I suppose he threw caution to the wind. He said once that the reason he went forward was because he saw the stewards circling. It could have been the case. That's like something Foley would come out with. Of all the lads, Kevin Foley.

———

I wasn't going nuts. We were back to a draw. We hadn't won the game. And my feeling was what the hell was I doing up there, I had better get back and defend. Which is what I should be doing.

—KEVIN FOLEY

The Dublin selector Pat O'Neill was standing up in the dugout, in pain because he had just rapped his head on the top of it, and shouting to his defenders to pull the player down, because the game was essentially over, and if they pulled him down the free would be useless.

A few yards away in the other dugout Seán Boylan had already decided that this was the greatest goal of all time, and two decades later he will not be dissuaded from that opinion. O'Rourke, being O'Rourke, described it as 'car-crash' football when he selected it for RTE's twenty greatest GAA moments. He told Foley that it was amazing he scored the goal of the year 'and you not able to kick straight.' But he wrote in his memoir that watching the replay of Foley's goal almost makes him cry.

Parents all over Co. Meath named their children Kevin in his honour, but the hero of the day was reluctant to talk about the goal that made history. He still is.

Liam Hayes articulated in the *Sunday Press* the collective shock of the Meath players at seeing Foley in this position. He had never scored, even in training. He was normally stopping them at the other end.

In fact, Foley would never have conceded a goal like the one he scored. Against Down in 1990 he prevented the goal that would have beaten Meath in the league final. He held Ciarán Duff scoreless in the Leinster final, Martin McHugh in the all-Ireland semi-final and Larry Tompkins in the all-Ireland final. He even held people scoreless when he was playing out of position.

He never raised a hand in celebration. Never allowed a smile. Just turned around and ran back into position.

Frank Foley told their sister sitting in the stand that Kevin had just scored a goal. She didn't believe him.

Nobody did.

––––

David Beggy was probably the cause of those four games. He scored the winning point, but he also made the point which levelled the first game with Dublin.

—P. J. GILLIC

Dublin were still thinking about the goal. John O'Leary's kick-out was won by Mattie McCabe and punched to Liam Hayes beneath the Hogan Stand. Hayes raced thirty yards, slipped inside Mick Deegan, looked up and decided to go for a point. For some unknown reason he changed his mind and lobbed the ball across the field to the only Meath player he could see, P J Gillic. Gillic gathered it under pressure. Everybody on the Meath bench was roaring, 'Shoot! Shoot! *Don't give it to Beggy. Don't give it to Beggy.*' They all believed that a ball kicked by David could go anywhere.

It mattered not that Beggy had got in the dispossession that led to the equalising point in the first match in the Deadlock saga, that he had scored a goal in the second match of Deadlock and that he had got lots of important scores for Meath in his innings. He was a rugby man, and it was as if they couldn't trust him fully. His approach involved a direct run on goal, getting close to the target and shooting over in a straight line—or into the net. From where he was, his team-mates believed, Beggy would never score.

———

Just as you have snobs in rugby, you have snobs in Gaelic. You have that hierarchical type stuff in Gaelic football: 'Sure what would you know about it, you're not a Gaelic man, your wife isn't in Macra na Feirme.'
—DAVID BEGGY, interview with Dermot Crowe,
14 January 2007

It didn't matter. In the tumult Gillic couldn't hear anyone telling him not to give it to Beggy. Nor had he any intention of giving it to Beggy.

All he saw was Eamon Heery coming to meet him. He was aware that there was a Meath player running alongside him. He had an idea. He lobbed the ball over the advancing Heery, secure in the knowledge that it would land in the hands of Bernard Flynn.

This, as it happens, was highly unlikely, as Flynn was safely on the bench, having been substituted by Mattie McCabe twenty-five minutes earlier. Gillic hadn't noticed. It was too late before he realised that he had, indeed, *given the ball to Beggy.*

Gillic says that when he saw who he had passed to he thought, 'Oh, shit.'

Beggy did what none of his Meath team-mates, then or now, thought he was capable of. He floated the ball delightfully over the bar, with style and panache—the winning point to end the Deadlock, and one of the most important scored in the history of the GAA.

Gillic didn't see it go over the bar. He had turned away, his head in his hands, sure that Beggy was going to send it wide, thinking, 'What am I after doing?' and wondering how he was going to explain it all to the rest of the boys.

Paddy Cullen, who experienced a brief surge of hope when he saw Beggy get the ball, wasn't sure where to look either.

> The biggest surprise of all was Beggy putting the ball over the bar for the winner. I would have settled for a draw. If you gave that ball to Beggy for a hundred years he wouldn't do the same thing.

Tommy Dowd was kinder.

> Beggy was a very under-rated player. He got an awful lot of important scores for Meath. He had great speed—it was just that his ball control mightn't have been brilliant.

———

We are within thirty seconds of the end of the most incredible series of football matches that were played in

any code the world over, ever. We have two seconds of
added time after the most incredible finale in any sport.
Is what we have just seen real?

—MICHEÁL Ó MUIRCHEARTAIGH's radio commentary for RTE1
of the closing stages of the fourth match

Dublin had one more chance, a final act of the drama, when
they were awarded a free sixty yards out.

It was too far out for a non-specialist kicker. Had Charlie
Redmond not been substituted he would have been there to
take it. Jack Sheedy opted in. He wasn't the regular free-taker,
but neither was anyone else on the field.

'It was just a matter of someone taking the
responsibility—or rather the blame. If it had gone over it
would have been a bonus.'

There was no sense in the ground that the Dublin free was
going to force extra time.

It might have dropped in the square into the jittery hands
of defenders and forwards. Instead, Jack Sheedy drove it high
and wide. What if!

———

The Dubs will forever see those matches as lost
opportunities, while for us it is the opposite.

—COLM O'ROURKE

What kept going wrong for Dublin? In August 1989 they
raced into a 1-4 to nil lead over Cork within fourteen
minutes. Then they were overtaken and had Keith Barr sent
off by half time. Cork made heavy weather of a four-point
win, 1-10 to 1-9.

In the first match of Deadlock their five-point half-time
lead was equalised in the dying moments. In the second they

were five points up with nine minutes remaining before there was a fisted goal by Bernard Flynn and two points from Brian Stafford. In the fourth match they were five points ahead half way through the second half and three points in front with only five minutes remaining.

Watching Paddy Cullen's face as he left the field it was difficult to know what he was thinking. He was inscrutable. I wonder what he said to the team in the dressing room afterwards? I wonder what will he do now? Who will he blame? Perhaps he should blame himself for making too many changes, for creating instability and uncertainty in the minds of his young players. Certainty is important to a team. They have to know what's going on, who to turn to for an idea and most importantly they have to know that their logic and reason are present in the dressing room.

—EAMON DUNPHY, *Sunday Independent*

Dublin used fourteen forwards in the series. Ciarán Duff complained afterwards that the management

switched things around too often . . . Generally it was the forwards who shouldered the blame, but were they the ones throwing away the big leads? . . . Take Seán Boylan as a contrast. He trusted his players, and even when the likes of Bernard Flynn and Brian Stafford were doing badly Boylan stuck with them, and it paid off.

The incredible saga lasted almost as long as four World Cup soccer finals, nine World heavyweight title fights and three Olympic marathons.

—MARTIN BREHENY, *Sunday Press*, 7 July 1991

Exhaustion. Everyone. Players, referee, fans, the media and the growing Gaelic football industry were exhausted.

Michael Lyster said to Paddy Cullen, the Dublin manager, 'You must be sick.' He replied, 'Sick is a good word. I can think of a better word.'

Cullen went in to give his congratulations in the Meath dressing-room: 'What can I say?' Meath players showed why they are good at the comeback: Gerry McEntee replied, 'Say it's free pints in Paddy Cullen's.'

'We robbed Dublin,' O'Rourke's analysis in the following day's *Sunday Tribune* went.

> They had the better of the game in all sectors of the field but they failed to put us away. Was this game enjoyed or endured by the players? I don't know. But I would not miss it for the world. I have seen it all now.

In his biography Hayes recalls being gripped by self-doubt. The intense satisfaction of beating Dublin was almost equalled by disgust at his own defeat in the middle of the field.

Sports writers too were exhausted. They found that they had little to say, or perhaps the enormity of what they had just seen was almost beyond description. In the *Irish Times*, Paddy Downey wrote:

> It was a game of extraordinary, sometimes bitter intensity. Some of the tackling was ferocious. The quality of the football was only moderate for much of the first

half but then it opened up and at times it matched the standard of the third match. Dublin left the field like broken men but as time passes they will realise and surely feel proud that they were part of the greatest, most riveting spectacle, in four instalments, ever staged in an Irish sporting arena.

They had gathered around Kevin Foley, asking if it was the best goal he had ever scored for Meath ('It was the only feckin' goal I scored for Meath!') and if it was unusual that he kicked it with his left foot ('I never kicked a ball with anything but my left foot').

The final word was left to the Dublin captain, Tommy Carr. It was the quotation of the campaign, the year and maybe the century: 'Football is more than football.' Everybody knew what he meant.

———

> The experience left us very much exhausted and tired and a little bit indifferent about what was going to come next.
> —LIAM HAYES

The Lord Mayor of Dublin, Michael Donnelly, had arranged a reception for both teams in the Mansion House. Tommy Carr was initially turned away because he had no formal invitation. He was eventually admitted, but he wondered why they we going to a civic reception when

> it was only four games of football, at the end of the day . . . There was no Dublin player really in the form for a civic reception . . . A civic reception meant we were celebrating something that had occurred. We had nothing to celebrate.

Liam Hayes insisted that his players should attend, however reluctantly. It was a gesture that was appreciated by Dublin. They were 'as drained as we were,' Jack Sheedy recalled. 'The only difference was that they had won.'

Opposition players of that era met after all-Ireland finals for a Monday lunch in the Burlington Hotel, where, in the pre-VCR 1970s, they watched recorded highlights of the match. This was the first such meeting for a match other than an all-Ireland final. Occasionally these were tense, such as the meeting after the 1988 final between Dublin and Cork. Hayes was determined that there would be no recurrence.

There was a near-farcical ceremonial element to the occasion. Liam Hayes and Tommy Carr were presented with Tipperary crystal vases. Hayes spoke briefly; Carr spoke for twenty minutes with passion. Hayes purposely made a very short speech.

> I didn't want to take up time, I didn't want to become in any way emotional and I didn't want to say too much. I didn't want to rub salt in their wounds by having anything like a celebration in their company. Carr looked like death, and yet he spoke with great conviction, without notes.

Colm O'Rourke recalled that 'Hayes said all the right things.' Tommy Carr spelled out very clearly the absolute devastation of losing.

> The whole thing came spilling out. Maybe I would be criticised for taking football too seriously. In terms of those games and what they said about the two teams, we had to take it seriously. We had to feel that much about it. We had to get involved emotionally and mentally in games like that. We couldn't but . . . Everyone wanted to

get away. The Dublin players were suffering badly, and the Meath players had far too much respect for what they had gone through to do anything but act in a most dignified way.

Charlie Redmond recalled that it was

> extremely difficult . . . We went back and they went back. They were in one corner initially, and they were in the other corner. And it was like a big divide. Over the period of about half an hour there was an intermingling with the players, and that sort of helped to alleviate some of the tension there was between the two teams.

———

Scene: The Meath dressing-room in the corner of the old Hogan Stand, near the junction with the canal end terrace. 6 July 1991, 22 minutes AD (after Deadlock).

Journalist: How do you feel?
David Beggy: Fucked.
Journalist: Do you feel anything printable?
Beggy: How about bollixed?

| AFTERMATH

The game has changed, players have changed.
Most of us are sick and tired talking about 1991,
and a lot of the younger players now haven't a
clue who we all are anyway.

—BERNARD FLYNN

The Deadlock was broken, so to speak, at 5:25 p.m. on Saturday 6 July 1991. It continues to be replayed in the imagination of everyone who was there.

When the final whistle was blown, Deadlock left the realm of football matches and was transformed into a social gathering. The players met first at the Mansion House, the Meath players silent and respectful and feeling out of place in the immediate aftermath of the encounter, the Dubs devastated.

They then met for golf outings, borrowing a tradition that Paddy Cullen had helped begin with the Dublin teams of the 1970s. They invited the referee, Tommy Howard, too, in case there was a dispute over the number of club lengths before the ball was dropped.

And yes, funerals. The premature death of Cork's John Kerins was the first. It brought Meath and Cork players together—players who hadn't spoken since the famous rivalry of 1987, 1988 and 1990.

The invitations to talk about 1991 declined. The guys had

tired of talking about it. Points instead of goals, cramps, eleven passes—it had stopped making sense.

———

You'd nearly want to be 10 points better to beat Boylan's men. And the further they went behind the better they got.

—BILLY KEANE, writer, from Listowel

Besieged Meath, bewildered Dublin. The counties assumed contrasting characteristics in the aftermath of Deadlock.

First the besieged. Thanks to Kevin Foley, the myth of Meath's triumphs in adversity was to endure and occasionally inspire.

Meath once had a Dublin fixation. Now Dublin had a Meath fixation. Dublin had held and lost a five-point lead on six separate occasions in the first, third and fourth matches. Meath's biggest lead was four points in the second match. The way the match turned out forged the perception of followers and media for a decade.

Seán Boylan later worried that so many comebacks, achieved so often, had affected his players' focus. Meath had begun to believe in their own indestructibility. Kevin Foley's was just one of a series of seemingly impossible Meath comebacks: Ollie Murphy in 2001, from six points down after forty-five minutes against Mayo in the 1996 all-Ireland final (eerily, they even had another equalising bounce, this time from Colm Coyle, which dropped between two Mayo and two Meath players and bounced over the bar); from six points down against Kildare at half-time in extra time of the 1997 Leinster semi-final replay (Boylan held firm against picking the star of the quarter-hour, Jody Devine, for the next match); and from nine points down after twenty minutes of the 2001 all-Ireland quarter-final against Westmeath. The mythology of Meath's indestructibility may even have extended to incidents such as Paul Bealin's missed penalty and Dessie Dolan's missed free, and to post-Boylan encounters such as the ball carried over the line by Joe Sheridan at the end of the 2010 Leinster final against Louth. One Louth fan even punched Boylan in the violent aftermath of that incident, probably for old time's sake.

There have been spectacular comebacks by other counties: Dublin came back from eight points down to draw with Kildare in 1994. The real comeback kings of football, Wexford, came back from eight points down in the second of Leinster football's previous four-match marathon, against Carlow in 1941, and then came from ten points down to beat Offaly in 1948. More recently, Wexford came from thirteen points down to beat Armagh in a league match in February 2005 and then came from eleven points down to beat Meath in 2008.

Long after Kevin Foley and Deadlock had passed into history, the myth of Meath's indestructibility lived on.

———

Meath didn't make it to the promised land in 1991. After ten matches, which was enough to win three in a row for the 1980s Kerry team, they lost to Down in the all-Ireland final.

They faced too many injuries with too little time to recover: Ferguson (groin), O'Malley (thigh muscle), Stafford (hamstring), Gillic (shoulder), O'Connell (collar bone) and Flynn (ankle). Colm O'Rourke came on in the final, and it looked like Meath were coming back again to snatch a draw or victory against the odds. They ran out of time.

'Underdog teams from the underdog nationalist communities of the six counties often lose just because they

play like underdogs,' the journalist Cormac McConnell of
Co. Fermanagh wrote on a visit to Co. Down before the
match. He recounted all the trappings of all-Ireland
qualification and the song by Danny Doran, 'We'll Bring
Back Sam Maguire', to the air of 'The Men Behind the Wire.'
The boys in red and black. The time of the novena in
Cloghogue church was changed by Canon Devlin on
Monday evening for the team's homecoming. It was changed
only three times before, for three all-Irelands and for
internment.

> For the men and women of Down, all trapped behind the
> wire, the football final in Croke Park is more, much more
> than just a game of football. No southerner can truly
> know how the men and women and children from
> behind the wire of their sad history will feel in Croke Park
> tomorrow. The signs on the outskirts of Newry this week,
> between the flags, screamed out: Money changed. Behind
> the wire, everything is changed.

This time Meath left it too late and missed by a paltry two
points, having come from eleven points behind. Down led
from the twentieth minute, and their fiftieth-minute goal
from Barry Breen proved to be their match-winner.

Colm O'Rourke came into the game ten minutes into the
second half. Mick Lyons retired injured half way through the
second half. A spectacular Liam Hayes solo-run goal got
Meath going, but they were still behind, 1-16 to 1-14, when the
referee, Séamus Prior, blew on the stroke of seventy minutes.
A Down fan who had climbed onto the roof of the Nally
Stand almost fell off when Hayes scored, Cormac's brother
Seán McConnell reported in the *Irish Times*.

Seán Boylan's wife, Tina, likes to tell the story of how she
turned up at the post-match function wearing red and black.

She was greeted with a combination of horror and disbelief. She really didn't understand this football business.

After the final whistle Liam Hayes cried. It had been eight years since he cried, and that was because of his brother's suicide. He had always assured himself that he could never cry after a game of football. 'I felt ashamed and angry. I quickly stopped. We had lost a damn game of football, and nothing more.'

————

Those games had a bonding effect, and it really annoys me any time silly comments appear about me or any of the Meath players having something against Dublin.

—COLM O'ROURKE

As one by one the Deadlock players retired, people began to ask if the famous rivalry between Dublin and Meath really existed, if it could really skip a generation. The answer is No. New rivalries emerged, Kerry and Tyrone grappling for dominance of the first decade of the twenty-first century prominent among them. Dublin and Meath proved to be nothing more than neighbourly oneupmanship, flickering rather than enduring, something each county has with the one next door. Were Meath's latter-day battles with Dublin more ferocious than those with Louth, Westmeath, Offaly and Kildare? Even in their heyday did they compare with the angry retributive clashes that Meath had with Cork and Laois? I think not.

Deadlock came and went, and the questions asked every time Meath were due to play Dublin grew more repetitive, the responses less introspective.

————

Liam McHale was on the receiving end of quite a number of blows. It was difficult having him sent off. I suspect if that hadn't happened we would have won the all-Ireland today.

—JOHN MAUGHAN, Mayo manager, after the 1996 all-Ireland final

Meath retained their reputation as the hardest hitters in the game. The 1996 championship landed the county and its tactics all over the air waves and newspaper columns, as the semi-final against Tyrone and the final against Mayo both broke down into savagery. In a new departure Meath's players found that they were being pilloried on RTE's 'Liveline'. Seán Boylan was blamed. He took it personally.

It is personal when you spend as much time as you do together. They realise my strengths, my weaknesses, and the fellows who are with me as well. Everyone goes out to play to their best. So some of the things that are written about you can hurt an awful lot.

You always think your team has been singled out when you do come in for it. We got terrible stick about the fight in 1996. It happened. What would you do about it? Would you turn your back and turn away from it? It is a difficult thing for fellows to know what to do.

One journalist friend wrote to me and asked what would he tell his eleven-year-old son. All you can tell him is that there was a row. It shouldn't have happened. It wasn't premeditated. It wasn't arranged. It just happened. These are amateur players.

The amount of tension that is around, that can change their lives so much, they do other things, and suddenly, this is the crazy thing, is that if you are defeated nowadays you are made to feel like a failure. Which of course fellows are not.

The length of the game is seventy minutes. We are the first to congratulate Mayo, if they beat us. We have always been good at that. But they can't blame us for winning. That's our job. That is what we set out to do, no matter how much people love to see Mayo win.

Wouldn't I love to see Mayo, not having won an all-Ireland since 1951? Of course I would love to see Mayo winning.

You couldn't go out with that on your mind, to do something. You'd be gone in two seconds, I'm not joking, because you would be distracted. If you go out that way you lose your attention on what you have to do.

In 1988 you are down to fourteen players after seven minutes, and you are playing against a team that had been defeated the previous year in an all-Ireland final. They were out to avenge that. You had to fight tooth and nail all over the park to try to survive. At one stage we're four or five points up and we barely survived. You had to keep going. You had to keep trying. A lot of people forget our players were getting hit as well. Badly hit in some cases.

———

There are many things about Boylan that are fundamentally different to most other GAA managers. A Ger Loughnane, Kevin Heffernan, John Maughan or Billy Morgan, Seán Boylan most certainly is not. For a start, he genuinely respects opponents and never bases his approach to big matches on personalised animosity. It's impossible to dislike Seán, let alone hate him. I'm glad he wasn't around in my day.

—EUGENE MCGEE

Seán Boylan carried on in the absence of his strong-personality players such as Gerry McEntee, Colm O'Rourke, Liam Harnan and Mick Lyons. In the 1990s the personalities were gone, but the younger players were more in thrall to him; he had total control over everything Meath teams did.

When things went wrong they did so spectacularly. Boylan criticised his players for their behaviour in their huge victory over Kerry in the 2001 all-Ireland semi-final.

> In the closing stages our fellows began showboating, slinging passes around for fun to the accompaniment of 'olés' from their supporters. This really upset me. If I learnt one thing over the years, it is that you never lose respect for your opponents.

It was the prelude to a spectacular collapse in the all-Ireland final against Galway that shattered all the illusions of Meath's invincibility. As the success became a distant memory, Boylan carried on, having, as a *Sunday Tribune* survey claimed, 'shaped how football, its good, its bad, its ugly was played for the guts of 15 years.'

Gerry McEntee expressed a real fear in Martin Breheny and Colm Keyes's book *The Chosen Ones* (2004) that Boylan could leave the team where he found it in 1982. Boylan stepped down in 2005 after twenty-three years at the helm and with Meath indeed at a low ebb. He's still in demand as a motivational speaker at Irish business events, and he's one of the few GAA managers to be instantly recognisable and instantly identified as a winner.

The independence gained from ditching our greatest
rivals in Leinster couldn't be underestimated.

DEGGIE FARRELL on Dublin's injury-time victory over
Meath in 1993

Despite the fact that Dublin won four subsequent Leinster
championships, their recovery was more complicated than
might have been expected. In 1993 Dublin achieved what they
had failed to do in 1991 and cast off the green hoodoo. As in
days of old, Meath came back from five points down to
equalise in the final minute. Jack Sheedy scored the winning
point in injury time.

It wasn't enough to exorcise the ghost of Deadlock. The
damage to their confidence in 1991 haunted Dublin teams
throughout the nineties. Tommy Carr recalled:

It was there for us to win in 1991 each day, particularly the
second, third or fourth day. The match against Derry in
1993 was even more Dublin's than Down's was in 1994.
Seven points up with twelve minutes to go. Or Cork in
1989, 1-4 to no score. We still lost the games.

According to Sheedy,

in 1991 we had a lot of momentum, a change of
management and a good deal of confidence ... There was
a swagger about us and we were playing good football.
Then it all came crashing down.

The series of prominent failures gave way to a new theory
that football needed Dublin to win an all-Ireland. They won
the all-Ireland in 1995. Tyrone are still infuriated by what they
see as a consensus that the GAA needed Dublin to win. The
theory that cost them victory didn't bear examination.

Nothing changed in Dublin GAA after 1995. It took many years to realise that the big change had come in 1991. With the new profile of the team came new expectations and new tensions. Even winning one all-Ireland didn't eliminate the expectation that Dublin should be winning every year.

'From 1991 onwards the profile of the team was so big that winning in 1995 didn't change a whole lot,' John O'Leary said. 'Until we beat Tyrone, Dublin lost only about three games out of seventeen, so we were involved in a lot of the bigger games all along.'

———

We almost made it. If we had got over Meath, we'd have won a few all-Irelands.

—PADDY CULLEN

Paddy Cullen made up for the failure of the Deadlock year by bringing Dublin to the 1992 all-Ireland final. When they failed to win, dramatically outplayed by Donegal, he left almost immediately, with a flash of cigar smoke and a joke: 'I'll be coming back to Croke Park for next year's final if I get a ticket.'

He said that he was 'under no pressure to go,' although nobody really believed him. It made sense that Paddy would go on his own terms. That was always the way it was going to be.

Instead it fell to Pat O'Neill to win the all-Ireland for Dublin after three more trying years. O'Neill departed in the afterglow of victory—a wise move, given subsequent events. The business of appointing Dublin's GAA manager had already become troubled by county-board politics and the accompanying media circus, and the transition from one manager to another occasionally bore more than a passing resemblance to Edward Gibbon's *History of the Decline and Fall of the Roman Empire.*

The succession list—nine since Heffo's second innings—was punctuated by ambushes and revolts, media leaks and vendettas. Pat O'Neill, 1992–5 (successful old-school disciplinarian and creator of Jayo); Mickey Whelan, 1996–9 (easygoing and unsuccessful, the subject of a dramatic player revolt, causing him to walk out after a league match); Tommy Carr, 1999–2001 (intense and dismissed by the county board despite being due another year and having strong player support); Tommy Lyons, 2002–4 (easygoing and unsuccessful, falsely promised the job in 1996 and the subject of a player revolt after the championship defeat by Armagh in 2003); Paul Caffrey, 2004–8 (intense and successful at the Leinster but not the all-Ireland level, beloved by fans and players alike, with his own nickname, 'Pillar', from his tendency to play with caterpillars when he was a child); and, incumbent since 2008, Pat Gilroy, a member of the St Vincent's *deirbhfhine,* which many suspected was directing Dublin managerial affairs from behind the scenes all along, as they had since 1949.

The expectations of success in Dublin GAA were such that they would certainly have led to Kevin Heffernan being removed as manager in 1973.

Cullen want back to a semi-celebrity lifestyle, loved by the fans, cordial and polite and welcoming to all comers. Himself and Jimmy Keaveney were omnipresent at major sporting events throughout the 1980s and 1990s.

The tribute of Dessie Farrell, among the harshest critics of Dublin management style, shouldn't be taken lightly. 'His attitude was to go out and enjoy the whole occasion. While he might not have been the strongest disciplinarian, he may have felt the players could have acted more responsibly.'

The voyage home through Dunboyne showed that
happiness and joy can be had without goods or riches.
—COLM O'ROURKE, in the week after the fourth match of
Deadlock, *Sunday Tribune*

The impact of Deadlock was always going to be greater in
Meath than in Dublin. About 20 per cent of the Meath
population attended the four matches; only 0.3 of Dublin's
population did.

The impact on Meath was also disproportionate. The
games enjoyed a surge at the youth level, and the county
could field 422 youth teams in 1997, compared with 178 in
1989. Dublin also increased their youth participation from
400 to 764. Expectations of success remained high, and
Meath went on to win championships in 1996 and 2000.

There was an inevitable downside. The Meath managerial
job became a poisoned chalice after Boylan's innings of
twenty-three years. In quick succession Eamonn Barry
(2005–6), Colm Coyle (2006–8), Eamonn O'Brien (2008–10)
and Séamus McEnaney had the job and the Damoclean
sword that went with it. O'Brien was voted out after winning
a Leinster title. The expectations in the county were such that
they would certainly have led to Boylan himself being axed in
1985.

Draw the games, draw the crowds and draw the cash.
—*Cork Examiner*

Some of the fans booed the referee at the end of the third
match, convinced that he had drawn the match for them.

They were beginning to resent the GAA system that endlessly replayed matches until one or the other team managed to win. Something similar happened after the second draw in the three-match series between Kildare and Meath in 1997.

The GAA said that this was mere coincidence and that replayed matches were neither a policy of the association nor, as was commonly suspected, an easy option for referees. Statistics have shown that, over the decades, neither teams nor referees have been conditioned to opt out when teams are level near the end of a match, and they show an increased tendency to finish a match when teams are level. Drawn matches have proved well worth the odds of the 12-1 on offer from most bookmakers.

The GAA championship was producing more replays than it had since the heyday of objections. (There were seven replays in the 1925 Connacht championship alone.) There were 50 drawn football championship matches in the 1990s, compared with 32 in the 80s, 28 in the 70s and 22 in the 60s.

But never was there a championship that approached anything like the replay record of 1991, when the Munster hurling final, Connacht football final, Ulster football semi-final and matches in Leinster were drawn in the first round (three replays between Meath and Dublin), the second round (one replay between Meath and Wicklow) and the semi-final (one replay between Laois and Louth).

The discretion of the referee in the playing of injury time lies at the heart of the problem. Questions about injury time are as old as the GAA itself. Wicklow were two points up against Meath when the sixtieth minute elapsed in their 1954 championship match. Paddy Meegan scored a winning point for Meath in the ninth minute of injury time, and Meath went on to win the all-Ireland. John Dowling allowed too much time in the 1966 Leinster final, then didn't allow Kildare to take a free at the end of the match.

The replay is at the heart of GAA culture. A century ago the sport of Gaelic football was established at the heart of popular culture when Kildare and Kerry met three times for the all-Ireland final. Another replay between the same teams in 1926, and three encounters between Cork and Kilkenny in 1931, provided the finance that built the earlier versions of Croke Park.

The 1988 Leinster football under-21 final had produced four draws between Offaly and Wexford at a time when attendances of 2,000 to 2,500 were the most that might be expected at Dr Cullen Park in Carlow. When the referee finished the third match after extra time with a draw—the third in ten days—the teams got a standing ovation from the crowd.

———

There was a bit of an inevitability about it, that it was going to go to a draw again. I think that got into player's minds and even the referee's mind, and at times you would think he was trying to balance out things.

—KEVIN FOLEY

Seven years after Deadlock a small but significant change of policy was made by the Leinster Council. It tested the theory that the GAA enjoyed an annual windfall of between £200,000 and £1 million from championship replays each year.

Until then, at all levels of Gaelic games in Leinster, in the event of a draw the referee was automatically reappointed as the referee for the replay.

Maybe because it has under its jurisdiction three of the most replay-prone counties in GAA history, the Leinster Council decided to appoint the referee in the case of a replay at the same time as they nominated a referee for the drawn match. The policy that made Tommy Howard a household name was no more.

This policy had given Leinster referees a reputation for applying apparently endless periods of injury time, allegedly in the hope of another day out, something that earned them nicknames such as the 'Equaliser' from the terrace wags.

But Leinster referees are not alone in enjoying this reputation. Paddy Collins, the chairman of the National Referees' Committee, denied that there is any temptation for a referee to 'play for a draw'; but privately many referees claimed that what one whistler described as 'abuse limitation' could persuade a referee to blow up when the scores were level at the end of a tense game.

Meath returned for more. In 1997 they won another mini-deadlock—three matches against Kildare—but lost their entire full-back line through injuries and suspensions before the Leinster final, in which they were outrun by Offaly.

Referees also complained that bringing about a replay could be a stressful experience. Pat McEnaney was pilloried for blowing up the drawn 1996 final with a couple of minutes to go. And it wasn't personally profitable. A decade ago Tommy Sugrue refereed a drawn all-Ireland final between Meath and Cork, a decision that yielded £600,000 for the GAA, but twelve months later he couldn't get two tickets for the all-Ireland final.

Then came the first big match of the 1998 championship under the new policy: Dublin v. Kildare. The result was a draw and a £350,000 replay for the Leinster Council.

Plus ça change ...

————

This was uncharted waters for our council or any other council. I am absolutely convinced that was the turning

point in Gaelic games being the attraction that they have
been in the past decade.

—MICHAEL DELANEY, Leinster Council secretary

Money. News coverage of Deadlock had quickly focused on
how much money was being generated for the GAA: £250,000
a match. 'Match three and win' was the introduction to
Miriam Lord's front-page feature about the third match. The
word 'bonanza' appeared in two dozen separate headlines
over five weeks.

The money didn't accrue to the GAA's central structures
(although the television rights, a not insignificant amount,
did); it went to the Leinster Council. Over the course of four
games they took in £1.1 million. Leinster had never generated
more than a million pounds in a championship season
before. Here was a first-round game that brought in
£1,111,898, and at the end of that season they had more than
£2 million.

By way of comparison, the Central Council's gate receipts
for 1990 amounted to slightly more than £2.3 million (out of
its total income of £3.1 million). The IRFU earned £1.3 million
from its two home internationals and £533,000 from renting
out Lansdowne Road to the FAI. The FAI had earned £2.5
million from World Cup qualifiers during the two years
before Italia '90, £900,000 from participation in the finals
and another £500,000 from home matches in the autumn
against England and Turkey.

More importantly this largesse was in the hands of the
most progressive of all the sections of the GAA: the Leinster
Council. They created a coaching structure, full-time
coaches, summer camps and the first major GAA investment
in something other than bricks, mortar and sods. It was those
1991 replays that created the generation that plays on
Saturday.

The decision not to give grants for county grounds was reversed. Instead, in 1991 Leinster gave a £30,000 grant to each of the counties in its jurisdiction, a contribution to the holiday fund of the two teams and development grants for Parnell Park and Cusack Park.

As one official remarked, 'While the GAA is not there to make money, it takes money to run the GAA. The more we get the more we give out.'

Meath, who lost their replay with Dublin in extra time in 1983 but who have won every major replay since, generated enough excess income to begin the redevelopment of Croke Park with their all-Ireland finals with Cork in 1988 and Mayo in 1996 and with Leinster championship marathons with Dublin in 1991 and Kildare in 1997.

But the real impact was the initiation of the GAA's first properly organised and funded coaching scheme. Summer camps were established throughout the province to engage with and train a new generation of players. The coaches included the Meath player Colin Brady.

Financial bankruptcy reflects a bankruptcy of idealism and of leadership.

—PETER QUINN

Provinces, or rather provincial councils, ruled the GAA for another ten years, but Deadlock had shown the GAA's Central Council how much it was missing by its not having access to important matches in the earlier rounds of the championship.

The £1.1 million series between Dublin and Meath in 1991 and the £1.06 million series between Kildare and Meath in 1997 provided funding for a major coaching initiative by the Leinster Council.

Of the combined provincial council income for 1997—
£7.8 million—half was generated by the Leinster Council,
which had seven gates of more than 40,000 during its
provincial football and hurling championships, counting two
replays between Meath and Kildare.

Leinster's wealth has been matched on occasion by
Munster, which also had a money-spinning hurling-final
replay in 1991. By contrast, two years earlier the council had
only one attendance of more than 30,000 in its hurling series.

The culture of replay windfall brings financial pressures of
its own. Replays show up the GAA's unhealthy reliance at the
provincial and the national level on gate receipts, which
make up two-thirds of its income at the national level and up
to 80 per cent at the provincial level. The Central Council's
windfall of £1.27 million from the 1996 replay—the
equivalent of the combined receipts for the four matches of
the Deadlock saga five years earlier—boosted income to
more than £8 million for the first time. Two-thirds of Croke
Park's income comes from gate receipts a greater
proportion than that of the leading English soccer clubs.
Before all-ticket finals and a back-door system gave the GAA
two meaningful semi-finals in the hurling championship, it
was vulnerable to weather and apathy: the combined all-
Ireland semi-final and final attendance in the 1979
championship was 66,000.

The hard-fought campaign for an open draw was
eventually won in 2001, and it at once moved the centre of
power away from the provinces to the Central Council.

Ten years after Deadlock, in 2001, the Central Council
enjoyed an income of €30 million, putting it just outside that
of the top 500 Irish firms. Increasing capacity to 78,000 has
moved it beyond that important benchmark.

While Liam Mulvihill was director-general of the GAA his
target was to boost commercial earnings so that the income

from gate receipts would be around 60 per cent. As gate receipts climbed he discovered something surprising: sponsorship options that hadn't been available before suddenly came into play.

——

Today amateurism is dead. No longer is money thought to corrupt. Instead, it has become every sport's life-blood. Its transfusions not only make thousands of sportsmen and women rich beyond the dreams of their predecessors, but they also pay for training facilities, modern stadiums, full-time coaching and efficient administration.

—*Economist*, 4 June 1998

Six years after Deadlock generated £1.2 million, the GAA in Dublin was facing bankruptcy. Ironically, while draws involving Dublin have generated more than a million pounds for the provincial council, the county board was facing a massive financial crisis of its own, which required £1 million to solve—a figure about equal to the gross yield from the Meath-Dublin series of 1991.

Dublin GAA wasn't benefiting from the large crowds generated by the county team's involvement in major competitions and was instead making lots of money for Leinster and the Central Council. The local championship didn't attract large attendances and generated very little revenue for the county board.

The Dublin County Board of the GAA was broke, and it had big challenges to face. It was in the front line in the three great challenges that confronted the GAA as a whole at the end of the twentieth century: rapid urbanisation, the spread of rival codes and the shortage of voluntary personnel to manage and organise the games. The sense of community and parish loyalty that inspired the GAA nationally had been swept away in the new urban environment, with its transient population and loss of identity. The ratio of clubs to population in Co. Dublin was the lowest in the Republic and second only to Co. Down in the country. Only Cos. Down, Antrim and Armagh—where circumstances militate against a higher club ratio—compare to Dublin's low number of clubs catering for a large population. 'Dublin County Board funds are drained by the fact they are largely left to face the problems of urbanisation alone by the GAA,' Costelloe argued in 1996 when he sought special assistance from the Central Council.

Their sponsorship deal with Arnott's depended heavily on inter-county success. In years when this didn't happen Dublin's huge financial headache got out of control.

A decision to redevelop Parnell Park gave the county a real alternative to the oversized Croke Park but also threatened to bankrupt the county board.

Dublin mourned that concerts—the salvation of Páirc Uí Chaoimh and Semple Stadium—were not an option. The reports of the county secretary, John Costelloe, to conventions of the 1990s repeatedly pointed out the irony of millions of pounds being diverted from the Irish market into licensing, sponsorship and merchandising income for English soccer clubs.

The problems didn't end there, Costelloe commented in the wake of the series of success and famous near-misses in the 1990s.

The ordinary club player in Dublin must be scratching themselves wondering where it all went wrong. While GAA has never had it so good, the most fundamental problem of all haunts our games at grass-roots level in the area where one in every four people live . . . Players train for matches which are postponed for weeks on end, months go by in the summer without a match, and a chaotic fixtures situation means that planning holidays, weddings or work patterns is an act of faith.

———

Eighty-thousand crowds at the height of summer masking an underpinning GAA that's tottering on the brink.

—MARK CONWAY, member of the Strategic Review Committee
that proposed splitting Dublin GAA in two, 2002

The Dublin conundrum continued to haunt the GAA. The 7 per cent market share that horrified Peter Quinn slipped further.

The GAA responded in 2002 by turning on the one aspect of the GAA in Dublin that had been successful: its identity. A proposal to divide Dublin into two county boards—Con Houlihan's response to the proposal was an ingenious two-word offering: 'Hill 8?'—was rejected overwhelmingly by fans and excited very little media support except from the former Offaly manager, Eugene McGee, a man who used the jackeen v. culchie rivalry to successfully motivate his teams in the 1980s. 'The attempt to split Dublin into two football counties is heading for a fast track journey to the bin,' Martin Breheny wrote. The *Irish Independent* had some fun with the proposal: 'First item on GAA agenda: the split.'

The committee criticised the notion that a Dublin all-Ireland win would generate a great growth in participation, calling it 'a dangerous top-down concept.' The reality is the opposite. The designation and operation of area-based GAA clubs would have served it far, far better. The committee also contended that the 1991 'saga' left more of a legacy in the media than anywhere else.

The creation of three separate local authorities out of Dublin County Council in 1994 (Fingal, South Dublin and Dún Laoghaire-Rathdown) brought the split back onto the agenda, and the GAA announced that a hurling team from Fingal would compete parallel to the main Dublin team in 2007, a move hoping to encourage hurling in the area. Players from the Fingal area are eligible for the main Dublin team, but the new team was entered in the secondary competitions the Nicky Rackard Cup in 2008, the Kehoe Cup in 2009 and Division 3B of the 2010 National Hurling League. The move created little excitement and wasn't seen as a threat to the boys in blue.

Mark Conway, a colleague of Quinn's from Kildress, Co. Tyrone, and a committee member in 2002, argued that

> the genius of the GAA is that it's all about place, about who you are and where you're from, about giving you the opportunity (and nothing else on this planet gifts people with that same vital opportunity) to make a statement about all those important things. Dublin is just far too big to give meaning to those concepts. It is far too big to manage, to administer ... With one Senior Football team representing a million people, you can't get the connectivity between supporter, member and player that we get in counties with a GAA population of less than a tenth of Dublin's.

Dublin GAA's biggest advantage was that it was on the doorstep of most of the country's biggest business enterprises, with sponsorship opportunities nobody else could match. The first casualty of its new foray into commercialism was its traditional Dublin 'three castles' badge, declared to be in the public domain by the High Court when the GAA tried to copyright it in 2004, as it was too similar to the coat of arms of Dublin City Council and the emblem used by other Dublin sports bodies. Dublin copyrighted a new GAA emblem.

In the new GAA world the past isn't a foreign country: just an unprofitable one.

––––

Every time Meath win, the shops and pubs make money. But there are ways of tapping into that. Who are they talking about making it?

—SEÁN BOYLAN

It was inevitable that all the talk of the Leinster Council's money during Deadlock would lead to the players wanting a slice of the action.

The GAA was already wrestling with the issue of professionalism before Deadlock. Raymond Smith of the *Sunday Independent* claimed that players were being paid for photo opportunities, with sums of £300 to £500 changing hands if they could get a photograph placed in a major newspaper.

The real pressure came from transfer arrangements. 'It's common knowledge that some Dublin clubs are paying players to join them,' John O'Leary declared in his biography. 'The bottom line is that professional-type transfers are happening in Dublin.'

O'Leary was right in saying that the business wasn't exactly secret. One St Olaf's player used his post-match speech to thank the people of Malahide for the new car they had bought him.

Managers too were being paid. It happened at the club

level, where it was assumed that a short-term pay-out would bring the success that a local side deserved. In the manner of these things it quickly careened out of control, with key managers able to put rival clubs in bidding matches against each other. The figures were not large, and they usually doubled as expenses and time in lieu of payments. Yet when he tried to investigate this illegal money trail the incoming GAA president, Peter Quinn, famously said that not only could he not find under-the-table payments, he 'couldn't even find the table.'

That didn't deter Liam Mulvihill from suggesting in his report to Congress in 1998 that payments to managers should be regulated, and Mulvihill's successor, Padraig Duffy, did likewise in 2010.

Paying players was more difficult. As attendances rose, the matter climbed on the agenda. Dessie Farrell of Dublin and the Gaelic Players' Association (which he established) denied wanting to push the association into full pay-for-play professionalism, but it was no longer clear where the boundaries lay.

Nine years after Deadlock the Austrian skiing team manager, Hans Pum, came to stay with Seán Boylan. He told him about the 103 members of the Austrian skiing team and the 55 people on the management; about how they went to the southern hemisphere during the northern summer and won the world championship.

He came to a Meath for a training session. He was enthralled by the fact that it was an amateur sport—that these were amateur players who played for their region, that they went to university or to work, that they met a few evenings after work and then at weekends, that they played against each other and then with each other, that there were no transfers, that no money passed hands and that there was an extraordinary loyalty to their club, their home and their county. He said it was an ethic you couldn't buy. For Boylan,

> if the game goes professional you could lose that ethic
> and a lot of the players. It sounds great getting paid. You
> are entitled to that bit of privacy, your own thing. But if
> someone is paying you, you are their servant.
>
> I know if I was getting paid, I wouldn't do the job I'm
> doing. I tell you that up front. Because there is a different
> onus on it then . . . Nobody owns me as it is. I'm a Gaelic
> man and that's it.
>
> Look after their expense and look after them well, but
> that's all. It's an amateur game. It is run by professionals,
> but every business is.
>
> If I see a player's association getting money, I want to
> see Jack O'Dowd who works with me and plays for the
> Dunboyne senior team, I want to see him looked after as
> well as the stars.
>
> A half dozen fellows walked in to fairly good jobs after
> we won the all-Ireland in 1996. Without the football they
> might have needed a marketing degree to get those jobs.
> Because they show on the playing field a level of work,
> commitment, dedication and so on, they are taken on.
> They prove themselves in their jobs. If they weren't
> playing football and had to go to university, they mightn't
> be guaranteed as good a job.

Boylan's approach was old school. Some of his players didn't
share it. 'Rounded up like sheep and left in the spare field'
was how Liam Hayes described it. According to Colm
O'Rourke,

> there were reports [that] three matches would make
> between £750,000 and £800,000 for the GAA. Here, I
> thought, am I, unable to move, sick with exhaustion and

for what? We are like the gladiators of old. We perform
for the entertainment of the crowd and, at the end of it
all, the only thing we get is a thumbs-up or a thumbs-
down.

———

Let us not be intimidated by abuse, ill-informed
comment, unsubstantiated allegations or self righteous
indignation, whether expressed in legislative assemblies,
on national television or in the local pub; whether from
headline-grabbers who move from bandwagon to
bandwagon, from controversy to controversy or from
scapegoat to scapegoat, or from well-meaning but naïve
do-gooders and compromisers.

—PETER QUINN's presidential address to Congress, 1992

While he talked traditionalist rhetoric the new GAA
president, Peter Quinn, had big plans for the association.
One of his first decisions was to curtail his own ambition. He
quickly realised that he could reform the association or build
a stadium. He couldn't do both. He opted for the stadium.

He knew that the great reforms in GAA history were
steered through by people who often opposed these reforms.
The opposition was immense and intransigent. At the
congress the Quinn motions were voted down one by one. In
time, many would be accepted, but the great reform he
envisaged was not.

The stadium was another matter. A near-disastrous crush
at the 1983 all-Ireland final, the steward's inability to handle
the gates at the 1984 Leinster final and the collapse of a wall
at the back of the Hogan Stand at the 1985 all-Ireland hurling
final, which injured two spectators, had all convinced the
GAA management that their coveted stadium would

effectually have to be rebuilt. Hill 16, the most urgent priority, was reconstructed in 1988. But big decisions had to be made, particularly as the consultants hired by Quinn told him that there was no prospect of covering the cost of the stadium from corporate sales.

The GAA needed bigger attendances than those on offer in 1991: a paltry 28,157 at the Leinster final between Meath and Laois, 40,166 at the all-Ireland semi-final between Down and Kerry, and 38,246 at the semi-final between Meath and Roscommon. The Cork v. Galway semi-final attendance in 1989 was even lower: 20,229. Levels like that would make the redevelopment of Croke Park impossible. It would bankrupt the association.

The Deadlock series showed that bigger attendances were possible with a higher profile. And a sustained high profile would give the GAA access to an untapped corporate market.

Did that market exist? With £150,000 for a single box and £250,000 for a double box the GAA was peddling an expensive and untried product. Quinn did what his business acumen had taught him: he hired another consultant. The second consultant told him to go ahead.

Building on an inner-city site, with planning difficulties and deteriorating relations with the local residents, costs more than twice what it would cost to develop a greenfield site.

Yet the GAA's first decision was to stand by its ground. It couldn't move out of a shrine. Croke Park isn't just a sporting venue: it's also the site where thirteen people were killed on Bloody Sunday in 1920, including the player after whom the Hogan Stand is named, Michael Hogan. Anyway, the race to greenfield sites, begun so enthusiastically in the USA in the 1960s, was being reversed in the 1990s by town planners and architects who were aware of the importance of stadiums in keeping urban areas alive, and of the importance of sport in keeping inner cities alive. The decision—an equally controversial one—was to phase the development to allow matches to be played throughout the period of development on what was essentially a building site.

Five acres behind the Cusack Stand were purchased from Belvedere College in 1990, and the final planning hurdles were cleared in two years, enabling the redevelopment to begin in 1993. The following summer, as the Cusack Stand took shape, the economist Kevin Gardner published the first document to use the term 'Celtic Tiger.' All the corporate boxes on the New Stand side were sold before the stand was opened in June 1996, as were the £5,000 ten-year premium seats.

The financial journalist Des Crowley, in an article in *Magill* in 1999, referred to the GAA scheme as 'the original Celtic Tiger.'

The project took seven years—three years less than anticipated. The pitch was realigned slightly to run parallel to the new Cusack Stand, eliminating what was a tight fit at the corner of the Nally and Hogan Stands.

In 2001 the project was completed, increasing the capacity of Croke Park to 82,000. The average attendance in the 2002 championship season was 55,000. When the Aviva Stadium was being built on the site of the former Landsdowne Road stadium, Croke Park hosted the record attendance for a soccer international in Ireland (73,160 at a World Cup play-off between Ireland and France in 2009), for a rugby international in Ireland (82,206 at Ireland v. England in the 2009 Six Nations Championship) and for a regional or club rugby match in Europe (82,208 at Munster v. Leinster in the 2009 European Cup semi-final).

Without the 1991 Deadlock, that decision to rebuild Croke Park would never have been made.

The Meath teams I had were a very honourable bunch of men who played it fair, played it hard and played within the rules.

—SEÁN BOYLAN

The GAA continued to make up the rules as it went along, and it was dumping referees in the same situation that Séamus Aldridge was dumped in in 1982 when he sent off John O'Keeffe. When new rules were introduced for a 1999 Leinster tie Niall Barrett, from Cork, dished out fourteen yellow cards, with four players sent off for Carlow. Westmeath won by four points.

The game was just as confused. It was also slowing down. According to Seán Boylan the Hanahoe rules, according to which sideline kicks and frees were allowed to be taken from the hand, had been the biggest change in the game in his lifetime. 'The whole emphasis for a number of years was to speed up the game. You had the situation where, when somebody got inured, play went on. Players got used to that.'

Then, surprisingly, it slowed down again with the introduction of yellow cards, red cards and ticking off.

The direct pick-up from the ground—in use in the women's game—failed to pass in 2005. The congress in that year opened up Croke Park to soccer, but it was a day of carnage for motions urging changes that would have rendered football faster and more attractive to spectators.

Boylan is happy that the game has progressed.

A lot of people are saying that skills are declining. If you stop and look back at matches that you can now see on television, there were some incredible ball skills. There is a big emphasis being put back on that now. You go mad on certain types of training. We are all guilty of it. If you are taking too much away from the rudiments of the game, you are going to lose out.

———

In a lifetime of sport I have never known a happier occasion. With all the talk of the international soccer team in recent years people have speculated about the future of Gaelic games. The GAA have nothing to fear. The wonderful character, the manners, the humour and the joy of the occasion matched for wonder the spectacle on the field. It was a good day to be Irish, a great day for the country's sport. On and off the field.

—EAMON DUNPHY, *Sunday Independent*, July 1991

In 1994 Ireland qualified for the World Cup finals once again. Some of the GAA's critics looked at USA '94 as another chance to marginalise a sport they disliked.

Declan Lynch described Croke Park as a good place to go to escape World Cup fever but said that you would be lonely there. His colleague George Byrne went further in condemning the

primitive pageant which will unfold in all its Neanderthal awfulness in Croke Park. The national games are only ours because any nation with a grain of civilisation running through its genes would rank them somewhere below the intricacies of dwarf-throwing or frog-swallowing. Bogball is in essence a free form exercise in pulling and dragging with a few rules and the limitless opportunity for physical violence.

While the fawning sycophants in the RTE sports department try to convince you that the foul-ridden farrago is part of what we are, it is part of what some of you are, that's for Desmond Morris to figure out, there'll be part of Dublin 4 which is forever betrothed to Sky Sports and the beautiful game, the absolute game, the world game, God's game.

Being from a centre city, working class background there's absolutely no way you would play bogball. Culturally we had and have far more in common with people from Liverpool, Manchester and London than some bunch of Clampetts from west of the Shannon, a fact often overlooked in the revisionist green-tinted view of Ireland. And yet, the Dubs phenomenon continues to thrive. Personally I love it when Dublin lose. I'm aware that the knuckle scrapers in every horrible hamlet beyond the Green Isle hotel love it too and I don't exactly relish the company, but it has to be said. In the main the people who follow Dublin are simply using the county's Gaah team as a surrogate Manchester United, Liverpool or Celtic.

The beautiful game, however, was still trapped in the fond memories of Mexico '70 nostalgicists. Though not as ugly as Italia '90, the USA '94 tournament failed to reach the heights of previous tournaments. Ireland's exit, with its farcical homecoming ceremony in the Phoenix Park, was in sharp contrast to the party atmosphere of what had gone before.

———

A lot of the imagination that kids have needs to be developed out in the open air, out in the fields. They don't get a chance to do it. I see young children at seven years of age getting an hour's homework. Madness, because they haven't got the concentration span. Other things will

suffer. It means that they are so tired they just sit in front
of the television.

—SEÁN BOYLAN

Newspaper editors, like army generals, tend to react to a new
challenge by pulling out their old plans. Having been caught
by underestimating the fervour of Italia '90, the papers were
determined to cover USA '94 properly as an event, not as a
sports tournament. The media all anticipated another Italia
'90. They didn't get one.

The GAA experienced something unexpected instead.
Gaelic football was growing on the back of soccer's
popularity. In 1994 and 2002, when youngsters were
animated by the World Cup, it was to Gaelic football
summer camps that they went. As football fever gripped the
country the youngsters who wanted to play weren't
particular about what sort of football they chose. In 1990 the
GAA didn't have summer camps for youngsters to turn to
when the World Cup gave a boost to field games of all kinds.
By 2002 they had fifty thousand kids involved and a hundred
coaches or games promotion officers working on the ground.
Huge numbers of new participants responded to the soccer
World Cup by signing up for GAA summer camps, made
respectable as a result of the funds generated by Deadlock.
Some of them saw increases of up to 40 per cent over the
previous summer.

At the time of Deadlock a survey by the Health Board
found that fewer than 50 per cent of fourteen-year-olds and
just under 20 per cent of girls took vigorous daily exercise. By
the age of sixteen it was only 14 per cent of boys and 8 per
cent of girls. After sixteen, it was down to 2 per cent for girls.

Teenagers were working part-time jobs in their spare time,
which once would have been spent playing improvised street
soccer or bashing a sliotar against a gable wall. They were

working for money that was then spent at the weekend on social activities, which rarely involve the playing of any sport.

Other surveys completed the picture: there was an alarming rise in diabetes relating to teenage obesity and the growth of a youth drinking culture. Pat Daly of the GAA described it as a time-bomb.

> The real issue is not whether kids play soccer, rugby or GAA. It is how sport is being programmed out of kids. We all have a problem trying to get them to play sport in the first place . . . The wheel is coming off in school sport. There is more and more pressure to do well academically and to spend more time at computers.
>
> Only 60 per cent of the 2,500 secondary schools have organised sports, and there are no firm statistics for the level of participation there.

By the end of the 1990s a more level-headed approach was being taken in tackling the serious business of sports participation in Ireland. Daly, Brian Kerr of the FAI and George Spotswood of the IRFU began to convene, not to dispute the merits of their particular codes but to get more young people off the couch and onto the playing field.

Morgan Buckley's strategic review of the state of Irish sport in 1997 showed an alarming drop-off in participation among teenage children, especially among girls. It wasn't just a GAA problem: it was a problem for everything, including rapidly expanding national waistlines and increasingly clogged national arteries.

———

Dublin against Wexford was a Saturday evening throw-in, and Ireland had played Cameroon in their opening

World Cup group game at 7:30 a.m. During the match that evening, five streakers invaded the pitch at different times.

—Leinster Council report, 2002

The GAA experience in 1990 informed its policy for World Cups to come and taught it to be less defensive. It learnt that once the tournament was finished things moved on quickly and returned to normal. Attendances at GAA matches, dropping for the duration of the tournament, shot back up. It also learnt that attendances at Irish soccer matches were less likely to benefit than Sky Digital's Premiership Plus season-ticket sales. According to Pat Daly,

> even if the country suddenly decided that they wanted to play GAA or soccer, and we all had an avalanche, we couldn't cope. We already have difficulties getting adequate personnel and getting voluntary people. We need to capitalise on the interest at times like this to invest in a system that can deliver to a bigger number of participants.

Irish people have learnt a lot from previous World Cups. We are a people who yearn for, and seize on, moments of collective experience. Hence our love of the sport—little practised in other countries—of jumping into fountains and our debate in 1994 over a homecoming party for a team that didn't make the last eight.

It proved that we don't love sport: we love parties.

————

The Hill 16 terrace was silent as the supporters stayed, sombre and stunned. It is doubtful if we will ever see the likes of this contest again. For the moment what can be said is, that at the end, rival players embraced and exchanged handshakes and jerseys. Only they can really tell what it was like. Time alone will tell whether the price paid by Meath for this historic victory will be worth the effort. What is certain is that neither side have lost caste or face. They have, however, learnt the admiration and respect of all.

—TOM HUMPHRIES on Deadlock

The media changed too. The taboo of live television for anything other than the all-Ireland semi-finals and final had been challenged in 1987 when the Munster hurling final was televised live. Live television of the fourth match had enhanced the Deadlock series. Four years after Deadlock, RTE had a full series of live matches, although the Leinster Council changed its mind in mid-1995 and decided not to allow its provincial finals to be televised, citing falling attendances.

By 1996 the debate was over. RTE's head of sport, Tim O'Connor, sat down with each of the four provinces and negotiated live television rights. The attendances had been driven down by the decision to start matches at 6:30 p.m. instead of 3:30 p.m., not by the fact the matches could be watched at home.

The 'colour' writing of the newspapers helped provide a wider vision of the event to the public. Miriam Lord and Fiona Looney moved into mainstream colour writing when they responded to the opportunities for word-play.

The series was a coming of age for Tom Humphries, the bard of Marino, who was to write with clarity and vision about the series and become a serial sports writer of the year in the coming decades. He was to give a Chandleresque edginess to the story, particularly in describing how those light blue and navy shorts affected the minds of an impressionable young generation.

Eamon Dunphy had stopped by and paid one of the most eloquent tributes of all.

> There will be no more wonderful day on our sporting summer, indeed there have been few contests as enthralling in sports history as this epic between old, weary champions and lean hungry young men fated to win but not knowing how. Meath don't know how to lose.

The traditional GAA writers were bemused—like boxing writers watching the arrival of Norman Mailer and the literary heavyweights at big fights in the 1960s—that their patch had been invaded by interlopers and literary drifters, as one was swept away by Deadlock as a metaphor for a nation in transition. They noted that many of those writing the eulogies had been condemning the GAA the previous summer, as they would again in December, when an unseemly row broke out over the staging of soccer and GAA in the same programme for a Fontenoy's promotion in the RDS. When the circus moved on, the traditional writers were the ones left balancing the myth and the reality of the Deadlock series. The newcomers were discovering things that their colleagues who spent every Sunday in the press box knew all along.

Those long-standing GAA writers were inspired too— inspired with the knowledge that there was a wider audience for them, waiting for them to make sense of something larger and more beautiful than most of them had ever realised.

GAA writing would never be the closed shop it once was.

——

Football is more than football.

—TOMMY CARR, after the fourth match of Deadlock

The four matches inspired others who were not even there—who had no idea of what was happening on those afternoons in Croke Park. The organisation of sport improved in the decades after Deadlock.

Some progressed faster than others: the 1992 Olympics were kinder to Ireland, with a gold and silver medal in the boxing ring. Athletics yielded a silver in 2000, and swimming three golds and a bronze—in controversial circumstances—in 1996. A report by the Department of Sport later that year set out the scale of the task facing Irish sport if it was to transform itself from a collection of well-meaning amateur bodies into something coherent enough to offer a serious level of participation to Irish people and to compete at the international level.

Irish sport was still underachieving because the Olympic movement wasn't sure what it was doing in these years. Various Government initiatives led to increased financial aid and a workable high-performance programme, but much of the money was sent to basically dysfunctional sporting bodies such as swimming, shooting and show-jumping. Grant-aided funding to all sport peaked at €143 million in 2008.

Rugby faced the biggest challenge of all when, rather inevitably, at the third World Cup in South Africa in 1995 professionalism was finally acknowledged. The game lost sixteen players almost immediately to well-funded English clubs and another sixteen in the summer of 1996.

Two of the old guard, Syd Millar from Ballymena and Noel Murphy from Cork, steered through a salvation plan, offering professional playing contracts with the provincial teams—three of them initially, and, reluctantly, Connacht as well. It meant subjugating the club scene and the all-Ireland league, which had briefly drawn large crowds in its initial years.

Ireland may not have managed to prop up the four proud provinces of its rugby anthem: three-and-a-half was as good as they could manage.

The participation of Irish provinces in the European Cup after 1995—and the successes of Ulster (1999), Munster (2006 and 2008) and Leinster (2009)—vindicated the policy. The rediscovered provinces were the nearest thing to a county GAA team in relation to sporting identity.

Despite a surge in popularity, renewed in 2002, soccer never escaped from the trap into which it had fallen with its exile team. The game was beholden to the big leagues of Europe, especially that of England. Fans travelled in large numbers to support foreign clubs—up to seven thousand in one airlift to Manchester United in 1998. Worse, the most promising teenagers emigrated before they had a chance to mature.

The repeated attempts of St Patrick's Athletic, Shelbourne and Bohemians to buy their way into the group stages of the Champions' League, and the raising of salaries—peaking at €3,000 a week and at Joe Gamble's €250,000 a year from St Patrick's Athletic, which was more than they would have commanded at top-flight clubs in Scotland and in the lower divisions in England—failed to lift the game from its historical penury. Many of soccer's problems derive from the fact that it remains the only major sport to be still partitioned.

The GAA showed that there was indeed a corporate market for Irish sport, and its example spawned a second big-capital project. The opening in 2010 of the redeveloped Lansdowne Road stadium gave soccer and rugby their own home. It cost twice as much as Croke Park—€411 million, with €191 million coming from the taxpayer. (Croke Park cost €180 million, of which €25 million came from the taxpayer.) Even with the extra grant aid, the size of the IRFU and FAI contribution threatened to engulf one or both organisations. But the scale of the ambition to provide a long-overdue facility couldn't be faulted.

The FAI in particular had lurched through several crises, a report on possible reform by the Genesis consultancy, a subsequent exodus and a high turnover of chief executives.

The GAA remained the largest sporting body in Ireland, with 2,600 clubs in Ireland and overseas: 230 in Connacht, 663 in Munster, 584 in Leinster and 807 in Ulster. It had 81 in Britain and 235 elsewhere in the world. The GAA had 14,511 youth teams playing throughout the country and about 83,000 young players. It had receipts of €70 million. The Dublin-Meath match in 2009 drew a crowd of 73,651, and the average attendance for its Croke Park summer championship fixtures was 61,200—more than the best-supported of the four matches between Dublin and Meath in 1991.

The potential that was first unlocked in those fixtures gave the GAA the vision and the courage to proceed to a new level. Everybody came along for the ride: the games at all levels, the family, the community, the city, the nation and the other sports that found inspiration of their own.

Devastated as those Dublin players were, and elated as the Meath players were, after that fourth match on 6 July 1991 their instincts were all wrong.

There were no losers from Deadlock: only winners.

We all got a trophy in the end.

Chapter 8 ∽

| EPILOGUE

The world turned upside down by four matches. Rewind.

Shocked Dubs. Exhausted players.

Beggy's point flying back to his boot.

Green flag flying. Foley, Dowd, O'Rourke, Dowd, Gillic, Foley, Beggy, O'Rourke, Harnan, McCabe, Lyons, O'Connell—Dublin leading by five with nine minutes to go.

Fans flying backwards through the entrance. The psychologist who thought it was a bad idea to bring the Meath team to Scotland.

The Leinster Council deciding a date for the fourth match before the third match was even played.

Four Dubs with cramp. Tommy Howard with cramp. No Meath men with cramp.

The ball hopping back over the bar to create the Deadlock in the first place.

Two names coming out of a jar at a Leinster Council meeting and everyone saying, *That* has never happened before.

Nor had it. Nor would Gaelic football be the same again.

| THE RECORDS

1991 LEINSTER CHAMPIONSHIP RESULTS

	Result	Venue	Attendance
19 May	Wexford 3-14 Carlow 2-7	Carlow	4,000
26 May	Louth 2-13 Longford 2-12	Drogheda	4,000
2 June	Meath 1-12 Dublin 1-12	Croke Park	51,144
9 June (R)	Meath 1-11 Dublin 1-11	Croke Park	60,960
23 June (2R)	Meath 2-11 Dublin 1-14	Croke Park	63,736
6 July (3R)	Meath 2-11 Dublin 0-15	Croke Park	61,543

Quarter-finals

9 June	Laois 1-17 Westmeath 0-6	Portlaoise	3,500
16 June	Louth 2-11 Kildare 2-10	Drogheda	15,000
16 June	Offaly 1-7 Wexford 0-7	Wexford	7,000
14 July	Meath 1-9 Wicklow 0-12	Croke Park	24,000
21 July (R)	Meath 1-12 Wicklow 1-9	Croke Park	41,215

Semi-finals

7 July	Laois 1-10 Louth 2-7	Croke Park	16,441
14 July (R)	Laois 2-14 Louth 0-12	Croke Park	24,000
28 July	Meath 2-13 Offaly 0-7	Croke Park	22,038

Final

11 August	Meath 1-11 Laois 0-8	Croke Park	28,157

ALL-IRELAND
Semi-finals
11 August	Down 2-9 Kerry 0-8	Croke Park	41,666
18 August	Meath 0-15 Roscommon 1-11	Croke Park	38,246

Final
15 September Down 1-16 Meath 1-14	Croke Park	64,500

PRIZE DRAWS
Gate receipts from big GAA marathons
1991   Meath v. Dublin
1st match	£235,372
2nd match	£262,363
3rd match	£314,623
4th match	£299,531

1993 Wexford v. Kilkenny
1st match	£173,487
2nd match	£219,867

1997 Meath v. Kildare
1st match	£330,631
2nd match	£355,171
3rd match	£388,546

Meath players used
Alan Browne	Kevin Foley	Gerry McEntee
David Beggy	P. J. Gillic	Mick McQuillan
Terry Connor	Liam Harnan	Martin O'Connell
Colm Coyle	Liam Hayes	Robbie O'Malley
Tommy Dowd	Seán Kelly	Colm O'Rourke
Terry Ferguson	Mick Lyons	Brendan Reilly
Bernard Flynn	John McDermott	Brian Stafford

Dublin players used

Keith Barr	David Foran	Joe McNally
Paul Bealin	Mick Galvin	Vinnie Murphy
Tommy Carr	Niall Guiden	John O'Leary
Paul Clarke	Gerry Hargan	Charlie Redmond
Paul Curran	Eamon Heery	Barney Rock
Mick Deegan	Ray Holland	Jack Sheedy
Pauric Doherty	Mick Kennedy	Declan Sheehan
Ciarán Duff	Donal McCarthy	Ciarán Walsh

2 JUNE

Meath 1-12	Dublin 1-12
Mick McQuillan	John O'Leary
Robbie O'Malley	Mick Deegan
Mick Lyons	Ciarán Walsh
Terry Ferguson	Mick Kennedy
Kevin Foley	Tommy Carr 0-1
Liam Harnan	Keith Barr
Martin O'Connell	Eamon Heery
Liam Hayes	Paul Clarke
P. J. Gillic 0-2	Paul Curran 0-2
Dave Beggy	Charlie Redmond 0-7
Colm O'Rourke	Jack Sheedy 0-1
Seán Kelly 0-1	Niall Guiden
Brian Stafford 1-4	Vinnie Murphy 0-1
Tommy Dowd 0-2	Dave Foran
Bernard Flynn 0-3	Mick Galvin 1-0

Subs

Meath:
Colm Coyle for O'Connell (59 mins.)

Dublin:
Paul Bealin for Foran (55 mins.)
Pauric Doherty for Galvin (59 mins.)
Ciarán Duff for Guiden (67 mins.)

9 JUNE

Meath 1-11	Dublin 1-11
Mick McQuillan	John O'Leary
Robbie O'Malley	Mick Deegan
Mick Lyons	Ciarán Walsh
Terry Ferguson	Mick Kennedy
Kevin Foley	Tommy Carr
Liam Harnan	Keith Barr
Martin O'Connell	Eamonn Heery 0-1
Liam Hayes	Dave Foran
Seán Kelly 0-1	Paul Bealin
Dave Beggy 1-1	Jack Sheedy 1-0
Colm O'Rourke 0-1	Barney Rock 0-8
Tommy Dowd	Ciarán Duff 0-1
Brian Stafford 0-5	Paul Curran
P. J. Gillic 0-2	Vinnie Murphy
Bernard Flynn 0-1	Donal McCarthy

Subs

Colm Coyle for Harnan
(51 mins.)
John McDermott for Dowd
(51 mins.)
Brendan Reilly for Kelly
(14 mins. ET)
Terry Connor for Gillic
(18 mins. ET)
Alan Browne for McDermott
(20 mins. ET)

Subs

Paul Clarke 0-1 for Curran
(57 mins.)
Gerry Hargan for Kennedy
(61 mins.)
Paul Curran for Bealin
(4 mins. ET)
Ray Holland for Barr
(19 mins. ET)
Pauric Doherty for Foran
(20 mins. ET)

Booked
Keith Barr
Mick Kennedy
Donal McCarthy (× 2)

23 JUNE

Meath 2-11	Dublin 1-14
Mick McQuillan	John O'Leary
Robbie O'Malley	Mick Deegan
Mick Lyons	Ciarán Walsh
Terry Ferguson	Mick Kennedy
Kevin Foley	Tommy Carr
Liam Harnan	Keith Barr
Colm Coyle 1-0	Eamon Heery
Liam Hayes	Dave Foran
Martin O'Connell	Paul Bealin 0-1
Dave Beggy	Paul Clarke 1-1
Colm O'Rourke	Jack Sheedy 0-2
P. J. Gillic	Niall Guiden 0-3
Seán Kelly	Declan Sheehan 0-1
Brian Stafford 0-10	Vinnie Murphy
Bernard Flynn 1-1	Barney Rock 0-3

Subs

Meath

Tommy Dowd for Gillic
Gerry McEntee for Kelly
P. J. Gillic for Hayes
Brendan Reilly for Foley
Seán Kelly for Dowd

Booked

Tommy Dowd
Martin O'Connell
Alan Browne

Subs

Dublin

Gerry Hargan for Walsh
(15 mins.)
Joe McNally 0-2 for Murphy
(44 mins.)
Paul Curran 0-1 for Guiden
(70 mins.)
Ray Holland for Kennedy
(0 mins. ET)
Charlie Redmond for Foran
(0 mins. ET)
Vinnie Murphy for Redmond
(HT ET)
Niall Guiden for Carr
(18 mins. ET)
Mick Kennedy for Barr
(20 mins. ET)

6 JULY

Meath 2-11	Dublin 0-15
Mick McQuillan	John O'Leary
Robbie O'Malley	Mick Deegan
Mick Lyons	Gerry Hargan
Padraig Lyons	Mick Kennedy
Kevin Foley 1-0	Tommy Carr
Liam Harnan	Keith Barr
Martin O'Connell	Eamon Heery
Liam Hayes	Jack Sheedy
P. J. Gillic	Paul Bealin
Dave Beggy 0-1	Charlie Redmond 0-5
Colm O'Rourke	Paul Curran 0-2
Tommy Dowd	Niall Guiden 0-4
Colm Coyle	Declan Sheehan 0-2
Brian Stafford 1-5	Paul Clarke
Bernard Flynn 0-2	Mick Galvin 0-2

Subs

Finian Murtagh for Padraig Lyons (14 mins.)
Gerry McEntee for Murtagh (30 mins.)
Mattie McCabe 0-1 for Flynn (46 mins.)

Subs

Ray Holland for Carr (49 mins.)
Joe McNally for Clarke (62 mins.)
Vinnie Murphy for Redmond (65 mins.)

APPENDIX

The speeches at the Mansion House by the opposing captains after Deadlock:

Liam Hayes: Thank you. To say anything more to Dublin would be patronising and incomplete.

Tommy Carr: What is a football match? What is the hype? What is the occasion? What is special? Football is more than football. It is about character. What you do on the field reflects what you feel about things. It is guys who will give everything, who will absolutely open themselves out, to show themselves to you. To show themselves to their comrades.

When I talk to my team I talk about character. What is it? It is such an easy word to say. An easy word to throw away. My God, those guys have it.

Some people here haven't been to more than ten games in their life. That doesn't matter. I hope they have seen, have grasped, have felt, what we put into the game. If we had won easily, I would be happy and some of you would be disappointed. Let's be practical. We play only to win, not to be exciting. Just to win. I always feel the same joy when putting on my jersey. I love this county. I would do anything for it. Thank you.

You have to keep your head up. You are still a man. You still have to meet people. You can't do these things when you win. I don't feel like playing football any more. This is my seventh year. I have lost every year. I don't like losing. I am a bad loser. I hate it. I make no apologies for that. I think anybody who isn't a bad loser doesn't put a hundred per cent into winning. I don't know where I go personally from here. I have to take each day as it comes for a while. I couldn't walk. Yet I will always ask myself, Did I really have to go off? Could I have persevered? I thought we had it.

I feel a certain amount of distress that they were able to walk the ball in as they did. I mean that just cannot be allowed to happen. But it did. You say to yourself, I wouldn't have let that happen. Thirty thousand people there said the same thing. But such things do happen. Those are the facts of the game.

INDEX

aggression and physicality, 42–5,
  47–8, 61–6, 106–8, 115, 126, 151
Aldridge, Séamus, 47, 80, 108, 174
Allen, Dinny, 91
amateurism and professionalism,
  168–71
Arnott's, 40, 165
Australia, international-rules
  series, 14–15
Aviva Stadium, 173

Barr, Keith, 64, 91
  Deadlock matches, 100, 102, 122,
    125–7, 130–31
  penalty, 130–31
Barrett, Niall, 174
Barry, Eamonn, 157
BBC, 13–14
Bealin, Paul, 91, 130, 148
Beggy, David, 11, 24, 77, 87, 88–9
  Deadlock matches, 105, 115, 118,
    123, 128, 135, 137–9, 145
  profile, 88–9
Benoit, Joan, 117
Billings, Dave, 96
Blatter, Sepp, 34
Bolger, James, 6
Bonner, Seán, 6
Boothman, Jack, 5, 29, 36
Boylan, Seán, 10, 41, 47, 56, 66–74,
  84
  aftermath, 147, 151–3, 157
  Deadlock matches, 103–4,
    114–17, 122–3, 127, 129, 132,
    134, 136, 141
  Meath identity, 51

profile and managerial skills,
  66–74, 77, 85, 152–3
on progression of game, 42, 168,
  170, 174–5, 177
Boylan, Tina, 149–50
Brady, Colin, 162
Brady, Colm, 77
Brady, Ger, 46
Breen, Barry, 149
Breheny, Martin, 8, 142, 153
Brennan, Shay, 37
Brennan, Willie, 76–7
broadcasting, 12–17, 180
Brogan, Bernard, 57
Brogan, Jim, 81
BSkyB, 15–17
Buckley, Morgan, 178
Burke, Mick, 66
Byrne, Frankie, 20
Byrne, George, 31, 175

Caffrey, John, 43, 46
Caffrey, Paul, 156
Carey, Pat, 112
Carley, Mick, 45
Carlow, 174
Carr, Declan, 90
Carr, Tommy, 5, 77, 85, 154, 182
  Deadlock matches, 100–102,
    113–14, 120–21, 131–2, 143–4
  manager, 156
  profile, 90–91
  speech after matches, 192–3
Carroll, Donal, 7
Carwood, Michael, 10
Casey, Bill, 45, 46

Cassells, Joe, 77, 104
Ceannáras, 5
Central Council, 162, 163, 164
Charlton, Jack, 28, 34, 35
Clarke, Con, 2, 39
Clarke, Paul, 67, 91–2, 114, 122
coaching scheme initiative, 162
Coghlan, Eamonn, 19
Cogley, Fred, 6
Cogley, Mitchell, 6
Cogley, Niall, 6
Collier, Pat 'Red', 66
Collins, Paddy, 160
'comeback kings', 148
Conlon, Marty, 38
Connacht championship (1990),
    29
Connacht Council, 4
Conway, Mark, 166, 167
Coogan, Fintan, 52
Cork, 44, 140, 146, 154, 159
Costelloe, John, 55, 76, 165–6
county grounds grant, 162
county panel, 84–5
Coyle, Colm, 43, 88, 147
    Deadlock matches, 114, 119–20,
        122
    manager, 157
Coyne, Tommy, 38
cramp, 116–17
Creavin, Liam, 114
Crofton, John, 102
Croke Park, 1, 92–8, 171–3
    crowd management, 93–8
    Hill 16, 59, 92, 94–6, 98, 172
    income, 163
    pitch condition, vii–ix
    redevelopments, 5, 171–3
        cost, 183–4
Crowley, Des, 173
Cruise O'Brien, Conor, 31–3
'culchie', 52–3, 56, 166

Cullen, Paddy, 40, 78–83, 155
    Deadlock matches, viii, 101–3,
        105–6, 110–11, 114, 116, 122,
        126, 131, 139, 141–2
    Dublin identity, 51–2
    player, 9, 55, 56, 78–80
    profile and skills, 78–83, 111, 146,
        156
Cummins, Brendan, 50
Cunningham, Bertie, 87
Curran, Paul, 91, 103, 104–5, 122
Currie, Sackville, 19
Cusack, Michael, 6
Cusack Park, 162
Cusack Stand, 5, 92–3, 173

Daly, Pat, 178, 179
Darby, Séamus, 56, 133
de Barra, Éamonn, 12
Deegan, Leslie, 56–7
Deegan, Mick, 11, 105, 120, 137
Deignan, Séamus, 40
Delaney, Michael, 23, 24, 27–9, 99,
    110, 118, 161
Derry, 154
Devine, Jody, 147
Devlin, Canon, 149
Devlin, P. J., 6
Dineen, Frank, 6
Doherty, Seán, 9
Dolan, Dessie, 148
Donnelly, Michael, 143
Donnelly, Shay, 46
Doran, Danny, 149
Doran, Paschal, 76
Dorgan, Val, 7
Dowd, Tommy, 10, 46
    Deadlock matches, ix, 105, 111,
        122, 135–6, 139
    profile, 88
Dowling, John, 158
Down, 148–50

Downey, Paddy, 7, 45, 121, 126, 142–3
Doyle, Bobby, 80, 81
Drumm, Tommy, 57
Drury, Fintan, 39
Dublin, 51–60, 61–4, 78–83, 90–92, 164–8, 176
county boards division, 166
fans, 96–8
finance, 39–40, 164–8
identity and economy, 51–5, 58–60, 166
local authorities, 167
penalty record, 130
physicality, 42–4, 61–4, 106–8, 115, 126
pool of players, 49–50
rural clubs, 62
sponsorship and logo, 1–2, 39–40, 165
team profile, 90–92
training, 116
youth teams, 157
1940s, 62
1950s and 1960s, 55–6, 62–3, 78
1970s, 44, 46, 56–60, 64–5, 79–80, 114, 119
1980s, 44, 57–8, 95, 130, 140
1980s v. Meath, 42–4, 61, 74–7
1990 v. Wicklow, 28
1991 statistics, 186–91
1991 v. Meath, 99–145
physicality, 43–4, 106–8, 115, 126
players and teamsheets, 188–91
1991–1999, 148, 154–7, 160
1993 v. Meath, 154–7, 160
2000s, 156, 178–9
Duff, Ciarán, 82, 92, 137
Deadlock matches, 101, 111, 113, 141

Duffy, Joe, 129
Duffy, Padraig, 169
Dunne, Mick, 6–7, 13, 77
Dunphy, Eamon, 35, 128, 141, 175, 181

Ellard, Michael, 8

Fahey, Frank, 18
FAI (Football Association of Ireland), 36–9, 161, 178, 184
Fanning, Pat, 1
fans, 96–8
contrast to soccer, 31–3
Farrell, Dessie, 97, 154, 156, 169
Fenton, John, 87
Ferguson, Des, 58, 71
Ferguson, Terry, 22, 87, 113, 126, 148
Fianna Fáil, 21, 53
finance, 4–5, 159–68
Finn, Jack, 126–7
Fitzgerald, Ciarán, 17
Fitzgerald, Séamus, 46
'Fitzgerald, Tommy', 7
Flaherty, Mary, 112
Flanagan, Oliver J., 52
Flynn, Bernard, 29, 86, 146, 148
Deadlock matches, 104, 115–16, 119–20, 128, 138, 141
profile, 89
Foley, Clíona, 14
Foley, Frank, 137
Foley, Kevin, 43, 89, 91, 147, 159
Deadlock matches, 124, 128, 132–7, 143
profile, 87
Foran, David, 101–2, 106, 116
Forbes, Mickey Joe, 64
Fortune, Michael, 8
fouls, 43–4, 47
Francis, Neil, 17

free-count, 43–4
Fulcher, Christine, 18

GAA, 1–5, 20–24, 168–84
  bankruptcy threat, 164–6, 172
  celebrates the past, 20–22
  coaching scheme initiative, 162
  congress (1990), 48
  congress (1991), 1–2, 20–22, 37
  congress (1992), 171–2
  conservatism and bureaucracy,
    2–3, 21, 31
  county panel, 84–5
  finances, 4–5, 159–68, 172
  growth, 20
  largest Irish sporting body, 184
  media and, 2, 5–17
  professionalism of players,
    168–71
  provincial councils, 4–5
  public relations officers, 10
  reforms, 171–2
  replayed matches system, 158–61
  rule changes, 46–9, 174
  soccer and, 26–39, 175–9
  sponsorship and, 39, 164, 165
Gaelic football, 42–50
  physicality, 42–5, 47–8, 61–6,
    106–8, 115, 126, 151
  professionalism, 168–71
  rule changes, 46–9, 174
  soccer and, 26–39, 175–9
  tactics, 44–6
Gaelic Players' Association, 169
Galvin, Mick, 92, 103, 106
Galway, 44, 68, 76, 153
Gardner, Kevin, 30, 173
gate receipts, 187
Geraghty, Graham, 10
Gillic, P. J., 87–8, 148
  Deadlock matches, viii, 105, 111,
    128, 137–9

Gilroy, Pat, 156
Ginnity, Fintan, 123
Gray, Jimmy, 23
Griffin, Liam, 51
Guerin, Denis, 44
Guiden, Niall, 91, 110, 111, 132

Hamilton, Fr Michael, 12
Hanahoe, Tony, 42, 47–9, 55, 57,
    80–81, 85, 119, 134–5
hand pass, 48, 49
Hanley, Dave, 12
Hargan, Gerry, 24, 82
  profile, 90
Harnan, Liam, 42–3, 76, 112
  Deadlock matches, 100, 106, 114,
    119, 134
  profile, 86–7
Hayes, Liam, 9–11, 42–3, 61, 65,
    85–6, 91, 149–50, 170, 192
  Deadlock matches, 100, 103–4,
    106, 124–5, 128–9, 131, 137–8,
    142–4
  profile, 87
Heery, Eamon, 43, 91, 121, 126, 127,
    138
Heffernan, Kevin, 56, 57, 63–5, 67,
    80–81, 101, 156
Hegarty, Declan, 19
Hendrick, Dave, 97
Hickey, David, 57, 64
Hickey, Donal, 1
Hickey, John D., 6, 63
Hickey, Paddy, 8
Hill 16, 59, 92, 94–6, 98, 172
Hogan, Michael, 172
Hogan, Vincent, 8
Hogan Stand, 92, 171, 173
Holland, Ray, 122
Houlihan, Con, 8–9, 25, 109, 166
Howard, Tommy, 64, 108–10,
    114–15, 122, 131, 146, 160

Humphries, Tom, 8, 33, 37, 108, 180–81
Hyland, Bob, 58, 65

Irish-language team lists, 3
Italia '90, 25–39, 161

'jackeen', 52, 166
Johnson, Tom, 71
Johnston, Trent, 38
journalism, 5–11, 65, 180–81
    Italia '90, 30–33

Kaliber, 39
Keane, Billy, 147
Keating, Noel, 41, 87, 123
Keaveney, Jimmy, 53, 55, 56, 78, 90, 156
Keenan, Donal, 7, 23
Kelleher, Robbie, 55
Kelly, Bill, 40
Kelly, Seán, 104, 111, 126
Kennedy, Danny, 13
Kennedy, Mick, 75, 90, 134
Kenny, Paul, 77
Kepak, 41, 50
Kerins, John, 146
Kernaghan, Alan, 38
Kerr, Brian, 178
Kerrigan, Jimmy, 86
Kerrigan, Mattie, 68
Kerry, 46, 84, 148, 150, 153, 159
Keyes, Colm, 153
kick-out rules, 48, 134–5, 174
Kildare, 71, 147, 158–9, 160
Kilfeather, Seán, 8, 32
Kilkenny, 159
King, Jim, 81

Laois, 27, 28, 76–7, 158
Larkin, Alan, 81
Lawlor, Liam, 112

Leahy, Georgie, 51
Leinster championship (1990), 27–9
Leinster championship (1991) statistics, 186–91
Leinster Council, 4, 5, 22–4, 28–9, 110, 118, 159–63
Lemass, Noel, 52
logos and sponsorship, 1–2, 39–41, 164, 165
Looney, Fiona, 180
Lord, Miriam, 161, 180
Louth, 148, 158
Lynch, Danny, 10, 32
Lynch, Declan, 30, 31, 33, 175
Lynott, Phil, 53
Lyons, Mick, 47, 76, 77, 88, 149
    Deadlock matches, 99–100, 102, 106, 130–31, 134
    sending-off, 114–15
    profile, 86
Lyons, Padraig, 87, 126
Lyons, Tommy, 97, 156
Lyster, Michael, 142

McAteer, Jason, 38
McCabe, Mattie, 77
    Deadlock matches, 128, 132–3, 134, 137, 139
    profile, 89
McCafferty, Nell, 30
McCarthy, Aidan, 7–8
McCarthy, Donal, 111, 115
McCarthy, Gerry, 7
McCarthy, John, 64
McCarthy, Mick, 35
McConnell, Cormac, 149
McConnell, Seán, 149
McCreevy, Charlie, 21
McCrohan, Owen, 107
McDowell, Liam, 7
McEnaney, Pat, 160

McEnaney, Séamus, 157
McEntee, Gerry, 66, 68, 153
  Deadlock matches, 99, 104, 122,
    142
  profile, 89
McGee, Eugene, 42, 67, 90, 152, 166
McGilligan, Brian, 86
McGinnity, Peter, 14
McGoldrick, Seán, 23
McGrory, Brenda, 18
McGuigan, Barry, 19
McHale, Liam, 151
McHugh, Martin, 137
McMenamon, Colm, 46
McNally, Joe, 82
  Deadlock matches, 101, 102
  profile, 92
McQuillan, Mickey, 77, 86, 113, 119,
    130–31
Mahon, Jack, 68
marking, man-to-man, 44–6
Marshall, George, 13
Martin, Séamus, 8
Maughan, John, 151
Mayo, 44, 147, 151, 152
Meath, 49–51, 65–78, 85–9
  identity and economy, 50–51
  indestructibility myth, 147–8,
    153
  physicality, 42–4, 61–2, 65–6,
    106–8, 115, 151
  pool of players, 49–50
  Scotland break, 123–5
  sponsorship, 40–41
  team profile, 85–9
  training, 72–3, 85, 116–17
  youth teams, 157
  1960s, 45–6, 66
  1970s, 66
  1980s, 44, 67–78, 86
  1980s v. Dublin, 42–4, 61, 74–7
  1990 v. Laois, 28

1991 final v. Down, 148–50
1991 statistics, 186–91
1991 v. Dublin, 99–145
  physicality, 43–4, 106–8, 115,
    126
  players and teamsheets,
    187–91
1991–1999, 147–58, 160, 162
1993 v. Dublin, 154–7, 160
2000s, 147–8, 153, 157
media, 5–17, 65, 180–81
  Italia '90, 30–33
Meegan, Paddy, 158
Mehigan, Paddy, 6, 7, 12
Millar, Syd, 182
Moore, Christy, 26
Moran, Dr Aidan, 123, 125
Moran, Kevin, 55, 110
Moran, Ogie, 77
Moran, Seán, 8
Morgan, Dermot, 35
Morrissey, Daniel, 52
Morton, Billy, 36
Mullins, Brian, 63, 64, 81, 118
Mulvihill, Liam, 1, 4, 11, 163–4, 169
Munster championship (1990), 29
Munster Council, 4, 22, 163
Murdoch, Rupert, 15–16
Murphy, Frank, 2
Murphy, Noel, 182
Murphy, Ollie, 147
Murphy, Vinnie, 43, 77
  Deadlock matches, 100–102,
    113–14, 131, 134
  profile, 92
Murray, Brian, 90
Murtagh, Finian, 89

Nally, Pat, 93
Nally Stand, 173
newspapers, 5–11, 65, 180–81
  Italia '90, 30–33

Northern Ireland soccer team, 26

O'Brien, Eamonn, 157
O'Brien, Frank, 50, 51
O'Brien, Mick, 68, 72
O'Brien, Paddy 'Hands', 45
O'Brien, Peadar, 7
O'Byrne, Arnold, 39
Ó Ceallacháin, Seán Óg, 7
O'Connell, Martin, 87, 113, 134, 148
O'Connor, Anne, 18
O'Connor, Cian, 19
O'Connor, Tim, 14–15, 180
O'Dea, Jimmy, 12, 52
O'Donnell, Tony, 79
O'Dowd, Jack, 170
O'Driscoll, Gay, 55, 57, 81, 90
O'Dwyer, Mick, 67, 120, 131
Offaly, 22, 25, 27, 28, 44, 63, 159,
    160, 166
O'Grady, Peadar, 62
O'Hara, Denis, 7
O'Hara, Paddy, 7
O'Hehir, Mícheál, 7, 12
Ó hEithir, Breandán, 21
O'Keeffe, John, 47, 174
O'Keeffe, Paddy, 7
Ó Laoi, Tomás, 12
Ó Laoire, Con, vii
O'Leary, Aisling, 18
O'Leary, John, 54, 77, 82, 86, 155,
    168
    Deadlock matches, viii, 104–5,
        115, 119–20, 122, 135–7
    profile, 90
Olympics, 18–19, 182
O'Malley, Robbie, 86, 103, 106, 148
Ó Muircheartaigh, Micheál, 12,
    133, 140
O'Neill, Colm, 46
O'Neill, Lucia, 112
O'Neill, Pat, 55, 63, 81, 96

Deadlock matches, 102, 111,
    116–17, 126, 130, 136
    manager, 155–6
O'Neill, Sadhbh, 112
O'Reilly, Gerry, 117
O'Reilly Transport, 40
O'Riordan, Tom, 82
O'Rourke, Colm, 51, 64, 66, 77,
    86–8, 90–91, 150
    Boylan and, 68, 69
    on changing game, 24, 43,
        170–71
    Deadlock matches, 99–100,
        102–4, 109, 112–13, 115, 122,
        126–7, 129, 134–7, 140
    final v. Down (1991), 148, 149
    newspaper work, 11, 69, 142, 157
    on physicality of game, 45, 75,
        107, 110, 127
    profile, 88
    training, 116–17, 124
Ó Síocháin, Seán, 7
O'Sullivan, Adhamhnán, 8
O'Sullivan, Dr Éamonn, 107
O'Sullivan, Jim, 7
O'Sullivan, Neil, 74
O'Sullivan, Sonia, 117
O'Toole, Anton, 75
O'Toole, Fintan, 21, 31

Páirc Uí Chaoimh, 165
Páirc Uí Rinn, 36
parentage rule, 37–8
Parnell Park, 162, 165
pay and professionalism, 168–71
penalties, 129–31
pitch condition, vii–ix
Power, Ger, 77, 79
Power, Paddy, 43
press and print media, 5–11, 65,
    180–81
Italia '90, 30–33

professionalism, 168–71
programmes, 118–19
Progressive Democrats (PDs),
    111–12
provincial championships (1991),
    23
provincial councils, 4–5
    income, 163
Puirséil, Pádraig, 6, 7, 56
Pum, Hans, 169–70

Quigley, James, 38
Quigley, Pat, 9–10
Quinn, Peter, 1, 2, 162, 166, 169,
    171–2

radio broadcasting, 12
Redmond, Charlie, 43, 51, 76, 77,
    85, 130
    Deadlock matches, 100, 103–8,
        110, 122, 130–32, 140, 145
    profile, 91
referee see Howard, Tommy
referees, replayed matches, 159–60
replayed matches system, 158–61
    financial windfalls, 159, 160–61,
        163
Reynolds, Pat, 99, 127
Robinson, Mary, 21
Robinson, Michael, 38
Roche, Pat, 65
Roche, Stephen, 19
Rock, Barney, 43, 75, 77, 82, 92, 95
    Deadlock matches, 101, 111, 113,
        115
    political candidate, 111–12
RTE, 2, 11–15, 180
rugby, 17–18, 59, 178, 182–3
    finances, 161
rules
    changes, 46–9, 174
    contradictions in rulebook, 3

Ryder, Fran, 56, 81

St Vincent's, 62–3
Sammon, Liam, 78
Scotland, Meath's break in, 123–5
seeding, 22–4
Semple Stadium, 165
Seoul Summer Olympics, 18–19
Shanley, Ollie, 46
Sheedy, Jack, 49, 54, 85, 154
    Deadlock matches, 102–3, 107,
        115, 119–20, 127–8, 140, 144
    profile, 91
Sheehan, Declan, 129
Sheehy, Mikey, 79–80
Sheridan, Joe, 148
Shouldice, Frank, 94, 95, 97
Siggins, Ger, 11
Sky Television, 15–17
Smith, Brian, 68
Smith, Raymond, 168
Smyth, Jimmy, 14
soccer, 25–39, 59, 175–9, 183–4
    finances, 161
sponsorship and logos, 1–2, 39–41,
    164, 165
Spotswood, George, 178
Stafford, Brian, 76, 77, 148
    Deadlock matches, 100, 104, 120,
        124, 129, 141
    profile, 88
Stanford, Ken, 18–19
statistics, 186–91
Staunton, Steve, 35
Sugrue, Tommy, 160
Sullivan, Cormac, 133
Sunday Tribune, 8–9, 11, 35, 153
supporters, 96–8
    contrast to soccer, 31–3
Sutton, P. P., 6
Synnott, Dave, 43

Taaffe, Fergal, 56
Taaffe, Tony, 112
tactics, 44–6, 100–102
Talty, Brian, 76
Tansey, Ben, 43
Taylor, Dennis, 19
teamsheets, 188–91
Teggart, Jack, 45
television, 11–17, 180
Tompkins, Larry, 137
Tormey, Bill, 112
training, 72–3, 84–5, 116–17
transfers, 168
Tyrone, 45, 64, 68, 95, 150, 151, 154–5

Ulster championship (1990), 29
Ulster Council, 4, 13–14
USA '94, 175, 176, 177

Vodafone, 40

Walsh, David, 8, 11, 61, 63–4
Walsh, Paddy, vii
Ward, Jason, 38
Westmeath, 45, 148, 174
Wexford, 44, 148, 159, 178
Whelan, Mickey, 81, 156
Whelan, Paul, 111
Wicklow, 28, 158
Wilson, George, 56
Wright, Myles, 54

youth participation in sport, 177–8
youth teams, 157

zonal systems, 44–6